Administrative Law

Foundations and Frameworks Series

A Clear Guide to Government Agencies, Rulemaking, and Regulatory Power

I.P. Werthausen

TME Press email: support@tme.net

Introduction

The rules that govern daily life in the United States fill more than 180,000 pages. Almost none of them were written by the people you elected.

Congress passes a few hundred laws in a typical year. Federal agencies issue thousands of rules in that same span. Those rules decide what goes into your food, how clean your drinking water has to be, what safety features your car needs, and whether the company down the street can release chemicals into the air. Congress wrote broad instructions like "protect public health" or "keep the workplace safe," then handed the details to agencies staffed with scientists, economists, and lawyers. Those agencies filled in the blanks, and the blanks turned out to be enormous.

Consider a single morning. The coffee in the cup cleared standards set by the Food and Drug Administration. The water that brewed it met limits from the Environmental Protection Agency. The car in the driveway was built to rules from the National Highway Traffic Safety Administration. The phone on the counter runs on airwaves the Federal Communications Commission controls. Four agencies touched one routine before the day even started, and not one of them answers directly to voters.

This is the world of administrative law. It is the set of rules that governs how agencies make decisions, write regulations, and enforce them. It determines the cost of your medicine, the safety of your job, and whether a factory can pollute the river near your home. Most people go their whole lives without learning how it works, even though it shapes their days more directly than almost any bill Congress passes.

Administrative law has a reputation for being dry. Law students often dread the course. Some practicing attorneys avoid the field entirely. Part of the trouble is that the subject sits in an odd spot. It is not quite constitutional law, though it leans heavily on the Constitution. It is not criminal law, though agencies can impose real penalties. It holds its own ground, and that ground touches nearly every corner of modern government.

The difficulty comes from a genuine tension at the center of the system. The Constitution set up three branches. Congress makes laws, the president carries them out, and courts interpret them. Agencies do all three at once. The EPA writes rules that work like laws. It enforces those rules through inspections and fines. It runs hearings that function like trials, with its own judges deciding cases. This mixing of powers is why some people call agencies a "fourth branch" of government, one the framers never put in the Constitution.

That tension is the reason the field exists. For more than a century, courts, Congress, and presidents have argued over how much power agencies should hold, what limits apply, and who gets to check them. The answers keep changing. A rule that stood for forty years can fall in a single Supreme Court term, which is exactly what happened in 2024 when the Court ended a doctrine that had shaped agency power since 1984.

This book is written for people who want to understand that system without a law degree. You might be a student facing your first administrative law course. You might run a small business trying to survive a permit process or an inspection. You might work inside an agency and want to see how your daily job fits the bigger picture. Or you might be a curious person who wants to know why so much of government runs through offices no one voted for.

Whatever brought you here, the aim stays the same. This book explains how agencies get their power, how they use it, and how that power gets checked. The writing stays plain. Legal terms get defined in ordinary words the first time they show up. Real cases and real agencies appear throughout, so the ideas stay tied to things that actually happened instead of floating in theory.

By the end, you will be able to read a news story about a new regulation and know what stage it is in and what comes next. You will know the difference between a rule and an order, between an executive agency and an independent one, and between the standards a court uses when it reviews an agency's work. You will understand why a company might sue over a rule and what its chances are. These are practical skills, useful whether you plan to work in law, policy, or business, or none of the above.

The book moves in a deliberate order, building from the ground up. Chapter 1 lays the foundation. It defines administrative law, separates it from constitutional and criminal law, and traces how the regulatory state grew from a few scattered agencies in the 1800s into the vast system running today. It introduces the fourth branch idea and the constitutional puzzle of whether Congress can hand its lawmaking power to agencies at all.

Chapter 2 looks at how agencies are built. You will see the split between executive agencies, which the president controls directly, and independent agencies like the Federal Reserve, which are designed to resist political pressure. It covers who runs these agencies, how they get appointed, and when a president can fire them, a question that has reached the Supreme Court more than once.

Chapter 3 explains where agencies get their authority. No agency can act on a whim. Each one draws power from a statute Congress wrote, called an enabling statute. This chapter covers those statutes, the Administrative Procedure Act of 1946 that set the ground rules for how every agency operates, and the role of presidential executive orders.

Chapter 4 gets into rulemaking, the process agencies use to write regulations. The main method, notice-and-comment rulemaking, requires an agency to publish a proposed rule, let the public respond, and weigh those responses before finalizing anything. You will learn why this process can drag on for years and how agencies speed it up during emergencies.

Chapter 5 covers what happens when an agency enforces its rules. Agencies hold hearings, employ their own judges, issue fines, grant and revoke licenses, and investigate suspected violations. This chapter follows an enforcement action from the first investigation to the final penalty.

Chapter 6 turns to the courts. When someone believes an agency broke the rules or reached beyond its authority, they can sue. This chapter explains who has the right to sue, the well-known Chevron doctrine and its end in 2024, and the test courts use to decide whether an agency's decision was reasonable or "arbitrary and capricious."

Chapter 7 examines the other checks on agency power. Congress holds hearings and can cancel rules it dislikes. Inspectors general dig into waste and abuse inside agencies. The Freedom of Information Act lets any person request agency records. Whistleblower laws protect employees who report wrongdoing. Together, these mechanisms expose misconduct, force agencies to explain themselves, and give outsiders a practical role in keeping administrative power accountable.

Chapter 8 puts the concepts to work in three specific fields: environmental regulation through the EPA, financial regulation through the Securities and Exchange Commission, and labor regulation. These examples show how the same legal framework produces very different results depending on the subject.

Chapter 9 looks ahead. It covers the questions the field is wrestling with right now, including how agencies use artificial intelligence to make decisions, the "major questions doctrine" that limits agency power on the biggest issues, and what agency authority looks like now that Chevron is gone.

After the chapters, the book gives you material to study and review. A historical timeline lays out the major events in administrative law in order. A set of example answers walks through the end-of-chapter questions so you can check your understanding. A conclusion pulls the main threads together. A list of key terms and definitions gives you a quick reference for the vocabulary. A works cited and recommended readings section points you toward the cases, statutes, and books worth reading next.

Each chapter closes with questions built to test whether the ideas stuck, and the example answers in the back let you check your work. You do not have to read the chapters in order, though the early ones build vocabulary that the later ones assume. If you are studying for a class, the chapters track the way most administrative law courses are taught. If you are here out of curiosity, jump to whatever interests you and follow the references back to the basics.

Administrative law rarely makes the front page, yet it decides more of ordinary life than almost any other part of the legal system. The rules that govern your food, your air, your money, and your job all run through it. Understanding how it works gives you a clearer view of how the government actually operates behind the headlines. Chapter 1 starts with the foundation: what administrative law is, and where it came from.

Outline

Chapter 1: Foundations of Administrative Law

- The Definition and Scope of Administrative Law
- Administrative Law vs. Constitutional and Criminal Law
- The Rise of the Regulatory State
- The Non-Delegation Doctrine
- The Three Branches and the Fourth Branch of Government
- Federal vs. State Administrative Law Systems

Chapter 2: The Structure of Administrative Agencies

- Executive Agencies vs. Independent Agencies
- Cabinet Departments and Sub-Agencies
- Agency Leadership: Appointment and Removal Power
- Organizational Charts and Internal Agency Hierarchy

Chapter 3: Sources of Agency Power and Legal Authority

- Enabling Statutes and Congressional Delegation
- The Administrative Procedure Act of 1946
- Executive Orders and Presidential Directives
- Agency Charters and Statutory Mandates
- Inherent vs. Delegated Authority

Chapter 4: Rulemaking Procedures

- Notice-and-Comment Rulemaking
- Formal vs. Informal Rulemaking
- Interim Final Rules and Emergency Rulemaking

Chapter 5: Adjudication and Enforcement

- Formal Adjudication Hearings
- Administrative Law Judges and Their Role
- Consent Decrees and Settlement Agreements
- Civil Penalties and Fines
- Licensing and Permitting Decisions

Contents

Chapter 1: Foundations of Administrative Law

In the summer of 1960, a drug company sent a routine application to a reviewer at the Food and Drug Administration. The drug was called Kevadon, and it had already sold well across Europe as a sedative and a remedy for morning sickness. The company expected quick approval. It got Frances Oldham Kelsey instead.

Kelsey, a physician and pharmacologist who'd started at the agency only weeks earlier, looked at the safety data and decided it wasn't good enough. She asked for more. The company pushed back, called her superiors, and complained about the delay. She held her ground and kept asking questions. Month after month, she refused to sign off.

The drug was thalidomide. In the countries that approved it, thousands of babies were born with severe deformities, many missing arms or legs. Kelsey's refusal kept it off the American market almost entirely. One government reviewer, exercising authority Congress had handed to her agency, spared the United States a tragedy that struck much of the rest of the world.

That story sits at the heart of what this chapter is about. Kelsey wasn't elected. She didn't write the law that gave the FDA its power. Congress had passed a statute decades earlier telling the agency to keep unsafe drugs off the market, then left the details to the experts. When Kelsey said no, she was making administrative law happen in real time. Her decision carried the force of the federal government, and no legislator voted on it.

This is how a huge share of American governing actually works. Congress sets a broad goal, an agency fills in the specifics, and the specifics shape people's lives. Understanding that arrangement, how it came to be, what powers it grants, and what limits hold it in check, is the work of this book. This first chapter builds the foundation. It defines the field, separates it from the areas of law people already know, traces how the modern system grew, and lays out the constitutional puzzle that runs underneath all of it.

The Definition and Scope of Administrative Law

Administrative law is the body of rules that governs what government agencies can do and how they must do it. It covers how agencies write regulations, how they enforce those regulations, how they hold hearings, and how courts review their decisions. If a bureaucracy touches your life, and one almost certainly does, administrative law is the framework that determines whether it acted properly.

That definition sounds simple, but the scope is enormous. The federal government runs more than 400 agencies, and every state adds hundreds more. These agencies produce the great majority of the actual rules Americans live under. Congress passes something like 200 to 600 laws in a two-year session. In that same period, federal agencies issue roughly 7,000 rules. The gap tells you where the real volume of governing happens.

Think about what these agencies control. The Environmental Protection Agency sets the limits on how much mercury a power plant can release. The Occupational Safety and Health Administration decides how much of a toxic chemical a worker can be exposed to over an eight-hour shift. The Federal Communications Commission auctions off the airwaves your cellphone depends on. The Securities and Exchange Commission decides what a public company has to tell investors before it sells them stock. Each of these agencies makes decisions that ripple through the economy, and each operates under the rules of administrative law.

Here's a useful way to picture the difference between what a legislature does and what an agency does. Congress passed the Clean Air Act and told the EPA to set standards that protect public health with an "adequate margin of safety." That's the whole instruction on the health question, more or less. It doesn't say how many parts

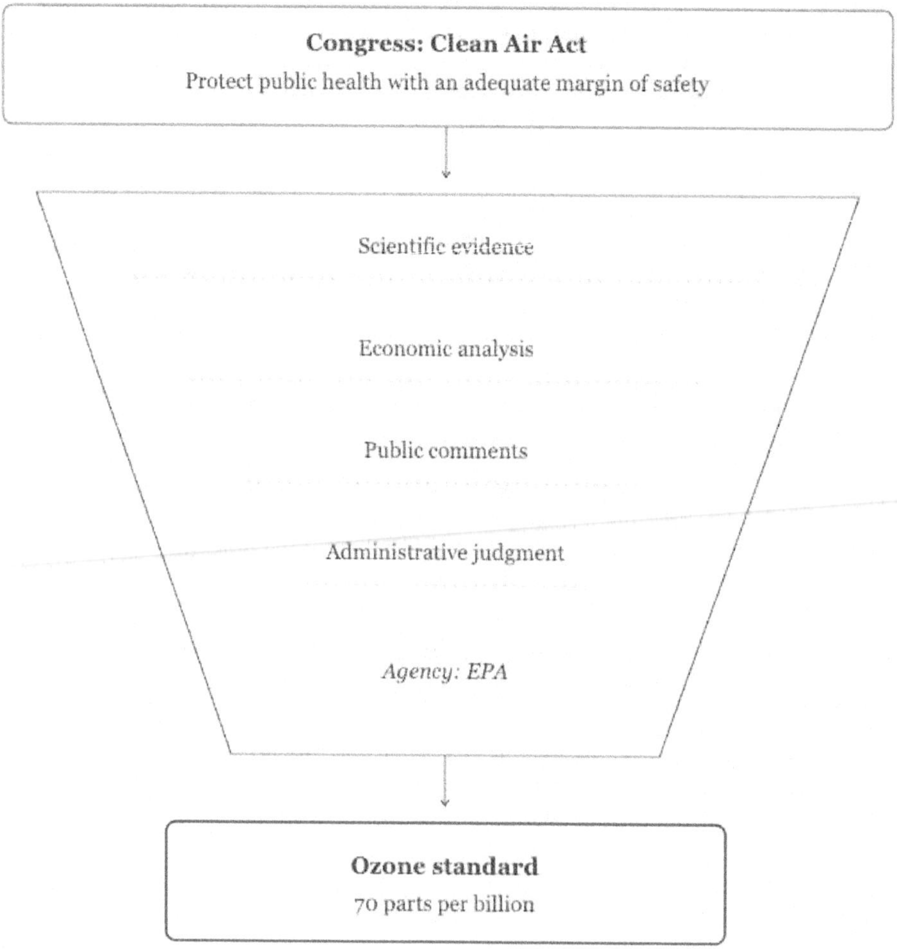

per billion of ozone are safe. It doesn't name the chemicals. It doesn't set the deadlines for cities to comply. The EPA does all of that. When the agency announces that the ozone standard is 70 parts per billion, that number came from scientists and administrators at the agency, not from a floor vote in the Capitol.

So administrative law asks a set of practical questions. Did the agency have the authority to issue that rule? Did it follow the right procedure? Did it give the public a chance to weigh in? Did it explain its reasoning? Was its decision reasonable, or did it ignore the evidence? Can a person who's harmed by the rule challenge it in court? These are the questions that fill administrative law casebooks, and they're the questions that decide real disputes every day.

Two main activities. Agencies do two big things, and it helps to name them early because the whole field organizes around the distinction. The first is **rulemaking**, which is how an agency writes a regulation that applies broadly to everyone in a category. When the FDA issues a rule that all packaged food must carry a nutrition label with certain information, that's rulemaking. The rule works like a statute. It's forward-looking, it applies to a whole class of people or businesses, and it becomes part of the code of federal regulations.

The second activity is **adjudication**, which is how an agency decides a specific case involving a specific party. When the National Labor Relations Board rules that a particular company illegally fired a worker for trying to organize a union, that's adjudication. It looks a lot like a court case. There's a hearing, evidence, a decision, and a party who wins and a party who loses. The difference is that the agency runs the whole thing, often using its own judges.

Nearly everything an agency does falls into one of these two buckets or supports them. Investigations gather the facts that lead to enforcement. Licensing decisions are a form of adjudication. Guidance documents help the public understand the rules. Once you can spot whether an agency is making a rule or deciding a case, a lot of the field snaps into focus, because different procedures and different standards of court review apply to each.

Where the rules come from. Administrative law itself draws from several sources, and they stack on top of each other. The Constitution sits at the base, setting outer limits on what any part of government can do. Statutes come next, especially the Administrative Procedure Act of 1946, which is the master statute governing how federal agencies operate. Then come the individual laws that create each agency and tell it what to do. On top of that sit the agencies' own regulations, plus decades of court decisions interpreting all of the above.

You'll notice this means administrative law is partly written down and partly built by courts over time. A student coming from a subject like tax law, where the answers mostly live in a code, sometimes finds this frustrating. Much of what matters here was worked out case by case, as judges decided how much deference to give agencies, when a person could sue, and what counts as a fair procedure. That case-built quality is a feature of the field, and later chapters spend a lot of time on those decisions.

The scope reaches further than most people expect. Administrative law governs the veterans' benefits system, which decides whether a disabled veteran gets a monthly check. It governs immigration courts, which decide whether a person can stay in the country. It governs the patent office, professional licensing boards, state utility commissions, and the agency that runs Social Security. Any time a part of the government makes a decision about your rights, your money, or your permission to do something, and that decision comes from an agency rather than a legislature or a regular court, administrative law is what's operating.

Administrative Law vs. Constitutional and Criminal Law

People new to this subject often struggle to place it, because it borrows from areas they already recognize without being any of them. Sorting out those relationships clears up a lot of early confusion.

Constitutional law deals with the structure of government and the rights the Constitution protects. It answers questions like whether Congress can regulate a certain activity, whether a state law violates free speech, and whether the president can act without congressional approval. Administrative law leans heavily on constitutional law, because the whole question of whether agencies can even exist, and how much power they can wield, comes from constitutional principles about separated powers. But administrative law operates one level down. It assumes agencies exist and asks how they must behave. A constitutional law question is whether Congress can delegate power to the EPA at all. An administrative law question is whether the EPA followed the right steps when it used that power.

The two overlap constantly. When someone argues that an agency's structure is unconstitutional, say, because the president can't fire its leaders, that's a constitutional argument raised inside an administrative law dispute. The Supreme Court has decided several cases like this, and they show up in later chapters. For now, the point is that constitutional law sets the boundaries of the playing field, while administrative law is the game played inside those boundaries.

Criminal law is where the contrast gets sharper and where a common misunderstanding lives. Criminal law involves the government prosecuting a person for an offense against society, with the possibility of prison and the protections that come with it: proof beyond a reasonable doubt, the right to a jury, the right to a court-appointed lawyer, protection against self-incrimination. Administrative enforcement looks similar on the surface, because agencies can punish people, but the protections are weaker and the stakes are usually different.

When OSHA fines a construction company for a safety violation, that's an administrative penalty, not a criminal conviction. The company doesn't face jail. The standard of proof is lower. There's no jury; an administrative law judge inside the agency usually hears the case. The company can appeal, eventually to a real court, but the process runs on administrative rules, not criminal ones. This distinction matters enormously in practice, because a business facing an agency enforcement action has fewer procedural shields than a defendant in a criminal courtroom.

The line can blur. Some conduct triggers both. A company that dumps toxic waste might face an EPA administrative penalty and a criminal prosecution by the Department of Justice at the same time. The administrative side handles the fine and the cleanup order. The criminal side handles the possibility of prison for the executives who ordered the dumping. Same underlying act, two separate legal tracks, two different sets of rules.

Laying the three areas side by side.

Feature	Constitutional Law	Criminal Law	Administrative Law
Core question	What can government do, and what rights are protected?	Did a person commit an offense against society?	Did an agency act within its authority and follow proper procedure?
Who acts	Courts, legislatures, executives	Prosecutors and courts	Agencies, reviewed by courts
Typical penalty	None (structural rulings)	Prison, fines, criminal record	Civil fines, license loss, cleanup orders
Standard of proof	Varies by claim	Beyond a reasonable doubt	Preponderance or substantial evidence
Decision-maker	Judges	Judge and jury	Administrative law judge, then courts on review
Main protections	Bill of Rights	Full criminal due process	Notice, comment, reasoned explanation, some due process

One more relationship rounds this out. Administrative law also connects to civil law, the branch covering disputes between private parties, like contracts and personal injury. Agency adjudication resembles a civil trial more than a criminal one, and courts sometimes borrow civil procedure ideas when they review agency decisions. But the resemblance is a family resemblance, not an identity. Agencies run on their own procedures, set mostly by the Administrative Procedure Act and each agency's own rules, and those procedures are the subject of this book.

The Rise of the Regulatory State

The system this book describes didn't exist for most of American history. The founders built a national government with no EPA, no FDA, no SEC, and nothing resembling the sprawling federal bureaucracy of today. For roughly the first century, the federal government was small, and most regulation, where any existed, happened at the state and local level. Understanding how the modern regulatory state grew explains why administrative law looks the way it does now.

The railroad problem. The turning point came with the railroads. By the 1880s, railroads had become the dominant force in the American economy, and they behaved badly. They charged farmers ruinous rates to ship grain, gave secret rebates to favored shippers, and used their monopoly power in ways that enraged the public. State laws couldn't handle a business that crossed state lines, and Congress didn't have the tools to write detailed rate rules for an industry that changed constantly.

So in 1887, Congress created the Interstate Commerce Commission, the first modern federal regulatory agency. The idea was new and a little radical: instead of writing every rule itself, Congress set up a permanent body of experts, gave it a mission, and let it regulate railroad rates on an ongoing basis. The ICC could investigate, hold hearings, and issue orders. It combined functions that the Constitution had seemed to separate, and it became the template for everything that followed.

The ICC struggled at first. Courts initially gutted much of its power, and it took later statutes to give it real teeth. But the model caught on, because it solved a genuine problem. Some subjects are too technical and too fast-moving for a legislature to manage directly. A body of specialists who work on the problem full-time can do what a part-time Congress of generalists can't.

The Progressive Era and the New Deal. Over the next several decades, the agency model spread. The early 1900s brought a wave of reform driven by public alarm over unsafe food, dangerous drugs, and corporate abuses. Upton Sinclair's 1906 novel about the meatpacking industry described conditions so revolting that public pressure helped push through the Pure Food and Drug Act that same year, along with meat inspection laws. The Federal Trade Commission arrived in 1914 to police unfair business practices. The Federal Reserve, created in 1913, took charge of the nation's monetary system.

Then came the transformation that built most of the modern state. The Great Depression of the 1930s convinced a large part of the country that markets alone couldn't be trusted to protect people, and Franklin Roosevelt's New Deal responded with an explosion of new agencies. The Securities and Exchange Commission (1934) took control of the stock markets after the 1929 crash wiped out millions of investors. The National Labor Relations Board (1935) took charge of union organizing and collective bargaining. The Federal Communications Commission (1934) took over broadcasting and telephones. Agency after agency appeared, each with power to regulate a slice of the economy.

This period generated fierce legal fights, because the sheer scale of delegation was unprecedented. Could Congress really hand this much power to unelected officials? The Supreme Court wrestled with the question throughout the 1930s, sometimes

The first was Panama Refining Co. v. Ryan, sometimes called the "hot oil" case. Congress had given the president power to ban interstate shipment of oil produced in violation of state limits, but it gave almost no guidance about when or why. The Court found the delegation too open-ended. A few months later came A.L.A. Schechter Poultry Corp. v. United States, the "sick chicken" case, which struck down a core piece of New Deal legislation. That law let industry groups and the president write "codes of fair competition" for whole industries, with barely any standards at all. The Court held that Congress had handed over its legislative power without meaningful limits, and it killed the program.

Those two decisions are the entire history of successful non-delegation challenges at the Supreme Court. Since 1935, the Court has rejected every attempt to strike down a federal law on non-delegation grounds, no matter how broad the delegation looked.

How lenient the test became. To see how forgiving the doctrine grew, consider the delegations the Court has upheld. It approved a law telling an agency to regulate broadcasting in the "public interest, convenience, and necessity," a standard so vague it could mean almost anything. It approved a law telling the price administrator to set "fair and equitable" prices. In 2001, in Whitman v. American Trucking Associations, the Court upheld the Clean Air Act's instruction to set air quality standards "requisite to protect the public health," rejecting the argument that this gave the EPA too much discretion. Justice Scalia wrote the opinion, and he made clear that the Court had almost never found a delegation too broad and wasn't about to start.

For decades, then, the non-delegation doctrine was mostly a museum piece. Everyone acknowledged it existed, and nearly everyone assumed it had no real force.

The doctrine stirs. That assumption has started to crack. In 2019, a case called Gundy v. United States gave the Court a chance to revisit the doctrine. The case involved a law that let the attorney general decide how to apply sex-offender registration rules to people convicted before the law passed. The Court upheld the delegation, but only barely, and the split was telling. Four justices signaled real interest in reviving a stronger non-delegation doctrine. Justice Gorsuch wrote a lengthy dissent arguing that the intelligible principle test had strayed far from the Constitution's design and that courts should demand more from Congress before letting it hand power to agencies.

Because one justice who might have joined that group didn't participate in Gundy, the issue was left unresolved, with a clear sense that the votes might exist to change the law. Since then, the possibility of a revived non-delegation doctrine has hung over the field. If the Court ever decides that Congress must write more detailed standards, thousands of existing regulations could be thrown into doubt, and Congress would face pressure to legislate in far more detail than it has for the last eighty years.

A summary of the doctrine's arc:

Case	Year	Delegation at issue	Result
J.W. Hampton v. United States	1928	Tariff-setting authority	Upheld; created "intelligible principle" test
Panama Refining v. Ryan	1935	Presidential ban on "hot oil"	Struck down
Schechter Poultry v. United States	1935	Industry "codes of fair competition"	Struck down
Whitman v. American Trucking	2001	Clean Air Act health standards	Upheld
Gundy v. United States	2019	Sex-offender registration rules	Upheld, but four justices signaled change

The non-delegation doctrine matters because it's the theoretical foundation for the entire debate over agency power. Every argument about whether an agency has gone too far traces back, one way or another, to the basic question of what Congress can hand off and what it must keep. Keep this doctrine in mind as the book goes on, because it's the thread that ties together many of the fights in later chapters.

The Three Branches and the Fourth Branch of Government

Every American learns the basic civics lesson: three branches, each with its own job. Congress makes the laws. The president enforces them. The courts interpret them. The design, drawn from the idea of separated powers, was meant to keep any one branch from getting too strong. Each branch checks the others, and power stays divided.

Agencies don't fit this picture, and that's the source of endless trouble. A single agency like the EPA does all three jobs at once. It writes regulations, which is a lawmaking function. It enforces those regulations through inspections and penalties, which is an executive function. It holds hearings and decides cases through its own judges, which is a judicial function. The Constitution split these powers among three branches on purpose, and agencies put them back together in one place.

This is why people call the administrative state a **"fourth branch" of government**. The phrase isn't in the Constitution. There is no fourth branch in the formal design. But agencies wield so much combined power, and fit so awkwardly into the original three, that the label stuck. Critics use it to argue that agencies are a constitutional problem, an unaccountable power center the founders never authorized. Defenders point out that agencies remain tied to the three branches in real ways and can't actually do whatever they want.

How agencies stay tethered. The "fourth branch" language can be misleading if it suggests agencies float free of control, so it's worth being precise about the leashes. Congress controls agencies through the laws that create them and the money that funds them. An agency can only do what its statute allows, and Congress can rewrite that statute, cut its budget, or abolish it entirely. Congress also holds oversight hearings and can cancel specific rules it dislikes.

The president controls much of the executive branch directly. For most agencies, the president appoints the leaders, sets priorities, and can remove officials who don't follow the administration's direction. Presidents also review major regulations before they take effect through an office in the White House, giving them a check on what agencies produce.

The courts control agencies through judicial review. When an agency issues a rule or decides a case, a person affected by it can usually sue, and a court can strike the action down if the agency exceeded its authority, ignored the evidence, or skipped required procedures. This power of review is one of the main safeguards in the whole system, and Chapter 6 is devoted to it.

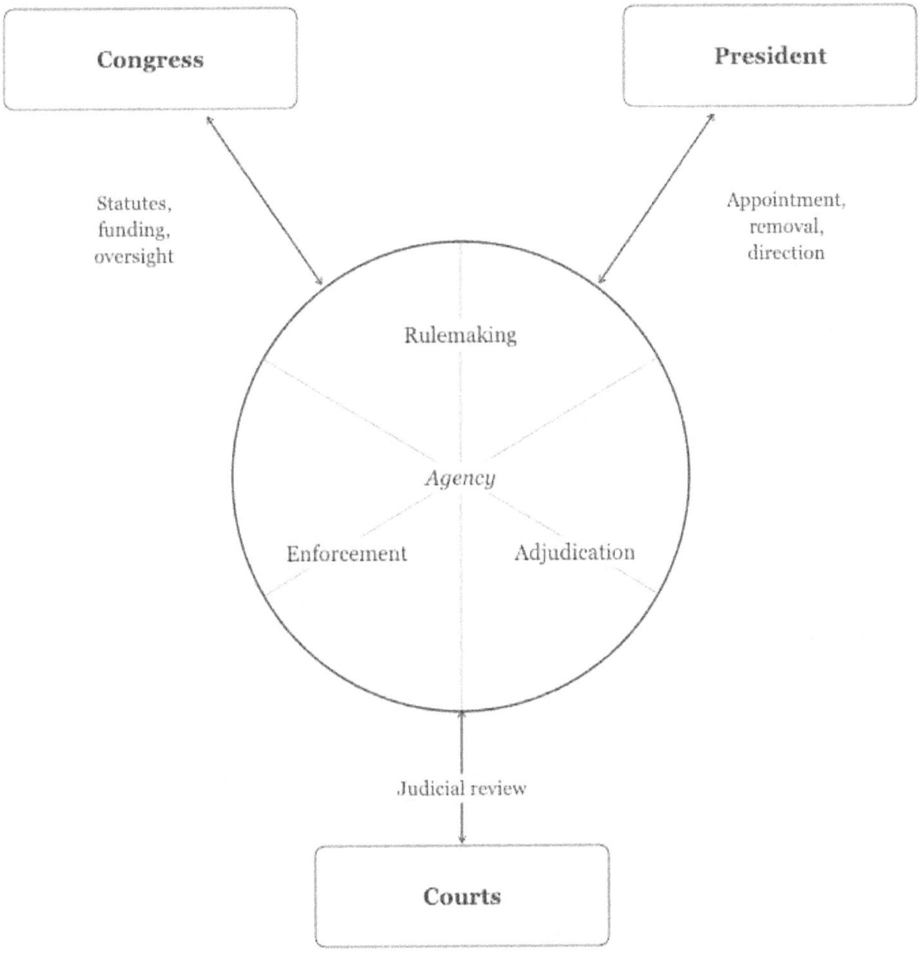

So agencies aren't a rogue fourth branch operating outside the constitutional order. They're embedded in it, checked from three directions at once. The "fourth branch" label captures something real about how much power they hold and how they combine functions, but it overstates their independence if taken too literally.

Why the tension never goes away. The reason this issue stays alive, decade after decade, is that the underlying tension has no clean resolution. The country wants expert agencies that can handle complex problems Congress can't manage in detail. It also wants government power to stay divided and accountable, the way the Constitution intended. Those two desires pull against each other. Give agencies enough power to be useful, and they start to look like a branch unto themselves. Restrict them enough to satisfy the separation of powers, and they lose the flexibility that made them worth creating.

Every major administrative law dispute is, at bottom, an attempt to manage that tension. How much should courts defer to agency expertise? How freely can the president remove agency officials? How detailed must Congress's instructions be? These questions don't have permanent answers, because the balance keeps shifting with the courts, the political mood, and the problems the country faces. The "fourth branch" is really a shorthand for a permanent argument about how to fit a modern administrative government into an eighteenth-century constitutional design.

Branch	Constitutional role	Chief power over agencies
Legislative (Congress)	Makes laws	Creates and funds agencies; can rewrite or abolish them
Executive (President)	Enforces laws	Appoints and often removes agency leaders; reviews major rules
Judicial (Courts)	Interprets laws	Reviews agency actions and can strike them down
"Fourth branch" (Agencies)	Not in the Constitution	Combines all three functions; checked by the other three

Federal vs. State Administrative Law Systems

Almost everything covered so far has focused on the federal government, but administrative law operates just as heavily at the state level, and the two systems run in parallel. Every state has its own agencies, its own procedures, and its own courts to review them. For many people, state agencies matter more day to day than federal ones, because states handle a lot of the government that touches ordinary life directly.

Consider what state agencies actually run. The department of motor vehicles decides whether you can drive. State licensing boards decide whether someone can work as a nurse, a barber, a contractor, or a real estate agent. State environmental agencies issue permits for local businesses. Public utility commissions set the electricity and water rates you pay. Zoning boards decide what can be built in your neighborhood. If you've ever renewed a license, contested a permit, or dealt with a state regulator, you've been inside state administrative law.

The structure looks familiar because states borrowed the federal model, but each state built its own version. Most states passed their own administrative procedure acts, many of them based on a model law that legal reformers drafted to give states a ready template. That model, revised several times over the decades, helped state systems look roughly similar to each other and to the federal system, though real differences remain. California, for example, runs a distinct process with a dedicated office that reviews state regulations before they take effect, a layer some other states don't have.

The two systems mostly stay in their own lanes, but they interact. Some fields, like environmental protection, use a cooperative arrangement where the federal government sets minimum standards and states run the actual programs, subject to federal approval. A state environmental agency might issue the permits and do the inspections, while the EPA sets the floor and steps in if the state falls short. In these areas, a business can find itself answering to both a federal and a state agency for the same activity, following two sets of rules at once.

One practical warning for anyone studying this subject: don't assume a rule you learned for the federal system automatically applies to a state. Standards of judicial review, procedures for challenging a decision, and deadlines for filing can all differ from state to state and from the federal baseline. A lawyer who handles a federal agency case can't walk into a state proceeding and assume the same rules apply. The concepts transfer, and this book gives you the framework that applies broadly, but the specifics always depend on which system you're in.

The relationship between the two levels reflects the basic structure of American government. Power is divided between the national government and the states, and administrative law mirrors that division. Federal agencies handle matters that cross state lines or fall under federal authority: interstate commerce, national securities markets, federal environmental standards, immigration. State agencies handle matters closer to home: local licensing, land use, state-chartered businesses, and the many services states provide. Both operate under the same basic logic this book describes, and the tools you learn here work in either setting, as long as you check the specific rules of the system you're dealing with.

Discussion Question

Frances Kelsey's refusal to approve thalidomide is often held up as proof that expert agencies protect the public in ways an elected legislature never could. Yet she was accountable to no voter, and her authority came from a Congress that had delegated the hard judgment to her agency. When an unelected official makes a decision this consequential, where should the line sit between trusting expertise and demanding democratic accountability, and does your answer change depending on whether the expert turns out to be right?

Chapter 2: The Structure of Administrative Agencies

A newly elected president walks into the Oval Office with a mandate and a long list of things to change. Some of those changes happen with a phone call. The president can fire the Secretary of Defense that afternoon and name a replacement by morning. The Secretary serves at the president's pleasure, and disagreement is reason enough.

Other changes hit a wall. That same president cannot fire the Chair of the Federal Reserve for cutting interest rates the wrong way. Can't remove a commissioner of the Securities and Exchange Commission for being too tough on Wall Street, or too soft. These officials sit inside agencies Congress deliberately walled off from that kind of direct control, and a president who wants them gone usually has to wait for their terms to end.

This split runs through the entire structure of the federal government, and it explains a lot about why some agencies swing hard with each election while others hold a steady course for years. It isn't an accident or a quirk. Congress made a series of deliberate choices about which agencies should answer directly to the president and which should keep some distance, and those choices shape how the agencies behave, who leads them, and how much a new administration can bend them.

This chapter takes apart the machinery. It starts with the biggest structural divide, the line between executive agencies and independent ones. It then looks at the cabinet departments and the smaller agencies nested inside them. It works through the constitutional fights over who gets to appoint and fire agency leaders, which is where a surprising amount of the action has happened at the Supreme Court. And it closes by looking inside a typical agency to see how it's actually organized, from the political appointees at the top to the career staff who keep the place running no matter who wins in November.

Executive Agencies vs. Independent Agencies

The federal bureaucracy divides into two broad types, and the difference comes down to one question: how much control does the president have? On one side sit **executive agencies**, which answer directly to the president. On the other sit **independent agencies**, which Congress designed to operate with some insulation from presidential control. The distinction sounds technical, but it drives real differences in how agencies act.

Executive agencies are the ones most people picture when they think of the government. They include the cabinet departments and many other bodies whose leaders serve at the president's pleasure. The head of an executive agency, whether a secretary or an administrator, can be removed by the president for any reason or no reason at all. If the president wants a new direction, the president installs new leadership, and the agency turns.

This gives executive agencies a defining feature: they change with administrations. When a new president takes office, executive agencies often reverse course, sometimes dramatically. The EPA under one administration might tighten pollution rules, then loosen them under the next, because its administrator serves the president and follows the president's priorities. That responsiveness is exactly what the design intends. Executive agencies are meant to carry out the elected president's agenda, and the tight leash makes sure they do.

Independent agencies work differently, and the differences are structural. Instead of one leader who serves at the president's pleasure, an independent agency is usually run by a group, a commission or board of several members. These members serve fixed terms, often longer than a single presidential term, and their terms are staggered so they don't all expire at once. Most importantly, they can't be fired at will. The statutes that create these agencies typically say a member can be removed only "for cause," meaning something like inefficiency, neglect of duty, or misconduct. Policy disagreement doesn't count.

Several features tend to travel together in independent agencies, and it helps to name them:

- **Multimember leadership.** A commission of five or seven members rather than a single head. The SEC has five commissioners. The Federal Reserve's Board of Governors has seven. The Nuclear Regulatory Commission has five.
- **Fixed, staggered terms.** Members serve set terms, often five, six, or seven years, arranged so that only one seat opens in a given year. This means a single president rarely gets to replace an entire commission.
- **For-cause removal.** The president can't remove a member simply for disagreeing with a decision. Removal requires a real reason tied to the member's conduct or performance.
- **Bipartisan balance.** Many independent agencies limit how many members can come from one political party. The FTC, SEC, and FCC all cap it, so no more than a bare majority can share the president's party.

Put these together and you get an agency that resists political pressure by design. A president can influence an independent agency over time by filling vacancies as they open, but can't seize control the way they can with an executive agency. That's the whole point. Congress created independent agencies for areas where it wanted expertise and stability to matter more than shifting political winds.

The Federal Reserve is the strongest example of independence in action. It sets monetary policy, deciding interest rates that affect the entire economy, and Congress went to unusual lengths to shield it. Beyond the fixed terms and removal protection, the Fed funds itself through its own operations rather than depending on congressional appropriations, which frees it from the budget pressure other agencies face. Presidents have often chafed at Fed decisions and complained loudly about them, but they've had almost no direct power to force a change. That insulation is why financial markets treat the Fed as a stabilizing force: its decisions aren't supposed to bend to whoever's in office.

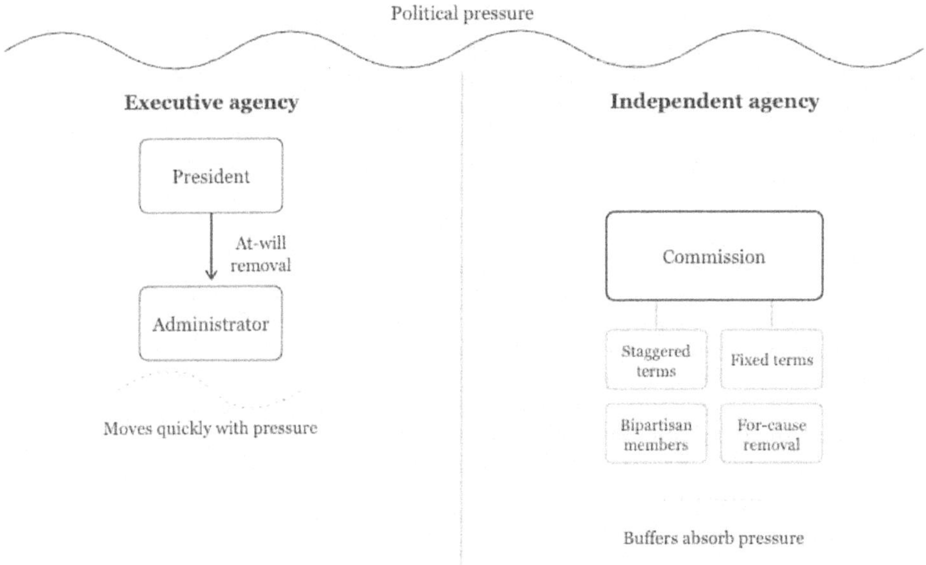

Feature	Executive Agency	Independent Agency
Leadership	Single head (secretary or administrator)	Multimember commission or board
Removal	At the president's pleasure, any reason	Only "for cause"
Terms	Serve as long as the president wants	Fixed, staggered terms
Party balance	No requirement	Often capped by statute
Responsiveness	Changes with each administration	More stable across administrations
Examples	Departments of Defense, Justice, State; EPA	Federal Reserve, SEC, FTC, FCC, NLRB

A word of caution about the labels, because they're slipperier than they look. The term "independent" gets used two different ways, and mixing them up causes confusion. Sometimes it means an agency that sits outside the cabinet departments, standing on its own in the organizational chart. The EPA fits that description; it isn't part of any department. But the EPA's administrator still serves at the president's pleasure and can be fired at will, so in the sense that matters most, the removal sense, the EPA behaves like an executive agency. The truly independent agencies, the ones with for-cause removal protection, are mostly the multimember commissions. When this book calls an agency "independent," it means the removal-protection sense unless it says otherwise.

The reason all of this matters goes beyond organizational trivia. Whether an agency is executive or independent tells you how it'll behave, how fast it'll change, and how much a new president can push it around. It also sits at the center of the biggest constitutional fights in the field, because the whole idea of shielding officials from presidential removal runs into the argument that the president is supposed to control the executive branch. That fight comes up later in this chapter, and the executive-versus-independent distinction is what makes it a fight at all.

Cabinet Departments and Sub-Agencies

The largest and most familiar executive agencies are the **cabinet departments**, the fifteen major divisions of the federal government whose heads make up the president's cabinet. These are the big ones, with names most people recognize: State, Treasury, Defense, Justice, and the rest. Each is led by a secretary (except Justice, which is led by the attorney general), and each secretary sits in the cabinet as a top adviser to the president. Together they employ millions of people and spend most of the federal budget.

The departments didn't all appear at once. They accumulated over more than two centuries, added one by one as the government took on new responsibilities. The first three arrived in 1789, the very first year under the Constitution: State to handle foreign affairs, Treasury to manage money, and War, which eventually became Defense. The others came later, each reflecting a new priority the country decided the federal government should handle. Agriculture, Commerce, Labor, and the rest each mark a moment when Congress decided a subject deserved a seat at the top table.

The most recent addition tells its own story. The Department of Homeland Security was created in 2002, in direct response to the September 11 attacks. It pulled together dozens of existing agencies scattered across the government into one massive department focused on security, in the largest reorganization of the federal government in half a century. Its creation shows how the cabinet grows: a crisis reveals a gap, and the government builds a new department to fill it.

Here's a look at the fifteen departments and roughly when they took their modern form.

Department	Established	A major sub-agency it contains
State	1789	Bureau of Consular Affairs

Treasury	1789	Internal Revenue Service
Defense	1789 (as War)	The armed services
Justice	1870	Federal Bureau of Investigation
Interior	1849	National Park Service
Agriculture	1862	Food Safety and Inspection Service
Commerce	1903	National Weather Service
Labor	1913	Occupational Safety and Health Administration
Health and Human Services	1953	Food and Drug Administration
Housing and Urban Development	1965	Federal Housing Administration
Transportation	1966	Federal Aviation Administration
Energy	1977	National Nuclear Security Administration
Education	1979	Federal Student Aid
Veterans Affairs	1989	Veterans Health Administration
Homeland Security	2002	Federal Emergency Management Agency

Sub-agencies are where the real work often happens. A cabinet department is rarely one unified body; it's a collection of smaller agencies gathered under one roof, each with its own mission, its own leadership, and often its own culture. The Department of Health and Human Services is a good example. Under its umbrella sit the FDA, which regulates drugs and food; the Centers for Disease Control and Prevention, which tracks and fights disease; the National Institutes of Health, which funds medical research; and the Centers for Medicare and Medicaid Services, which runs the giant health-insurance programs. These are wildly different operations, and each has enormous authority in its own right, yet all report up through the same secretary.

The Department of Justice works the same way. People think of it as one thing, but it houses the FBI, the Drug Enforcement Administration, the Bureau of Alcohol, Tobacco, Firearms and Explosives, the Bureau of Prisons, and the U.S. Marshals Service, along with the lawyers who represent the government in court. Each of these has a distinct job, and each carries a familiar name of its own, but the attorney general sits at the top of all of them.

This nesting structure matters for a practical reason: when you deal with the government, you're almost always dealing with a sub-agency, not the department as a whole. A drug company negotiates with the FDA, not with HHS in the abstract. A pilot answers to the FAA, not to the Department of Transportation directly. The department provides the overall structure and the cabinet-level leadership, but the sub-agency is the body that writes the rules you follow and makes the decisions that affect you. Knowing which sub-agency actually holds the authority is often the first step in understanding any regulatory problem.

Not every federal agency lives inside a cabinet department, though. Plenty operate outside the departmental structure entirely. The EPA stands on its own, reporting to the president without a department above it. The independent commissions like the SEC and the FTC sit outside the departments too. So the cabinet departments are the biggest and most visible piece of the executive branch, but they're not the whole picture. The government is a mix of departments with their nested sub-agencies plus a large number of freestanding agencies, some executive and some independent, that don't fit into any department at all.

Agency Leadership: Appointment and Removal Power

Who gets to put agency leaders in their jobs, and who gets to take them out? These two questions, appointment and removal, have generated some of the most consequential constitutional battles in American law, and the fights are still going. The reason they matter so much is that control over personnel is control over policy. Whoever appoints and removes agency leaders effectively controls what agencies do. So the rules about hiring and firing at the top aren't administrative housekeeping. They're a struggle over power between the president and Congress that reaches back to the founding.

The Appointments Clause. The Constitution addresses appointment directly. Article II says the president appoints "Officers of the United States" with the advice and consent of the Senate. That's the default: the president picks, and the Senate confirms. This covers the top jobs, called **principal officers**, which include cabinet secretaries, agency heads, ambassadors, and federal judges. When a president nominates a new Secretary of Labor or a new SEC commissioner, the Senate holds hearings and votes on whether to confirm. That confirmation requirement is a check on presidential power, giving the Senate a say in who runs the government.

But the Constitution creates a second, lighter track for lesser officials. It allows Congress to let **inferior officers** be appointed without Senate confirmation, either by the president alone, by the courts, or by the heads of departments. This makes practical sense, because the government has far too many officials for the Senate to confirm every one. So Congress routinely lets department heads appoint the lower-level officers who work beneath them.

The line between a principal officer and an inferior officer isn't always obvious, and it's produced its own litigation. The general test, refined in a 1997 case called Edmond v. United States, asks whether the official's work is directed and supervised by someone who was appointed with Senate confirmation. If a higher officer oversees them, they're probably inferior; if they answer to no one but the president, they're probably principal. The distinction determines whether Senate confirmation is required, which is why parties fight over it.

Below even the inferior officers sits a third category: ordinary **employees**, who aren't "officers" at all and don't go through the Appointments Clause process. Most federal workers fall here. The tricky part is drawing the line between an inferior officer, who must be properly appointed, and a mere employee, who can just be hired. The Supreme Court took this up in Lucia v. SEC in 2018 and held that the SEC's administrative law judges, the officials who preside over the agency's hearings, are inferior officers, not employees. That meant they had to be appointed consistent with the Appointments Clause rather than simply hired through the normal civil-service process. The decision forced the SEC and other agencies to change how they installed their judges, and it showed that the officer-versus-employee line has real teeth.

The removal power saga. If appointment is complicated, removal is where the constitutional drama really lives, because the Constitution says almost nothing about it. It spells out how officials get appointed but is nearly silent on how they can be fired, apart from impeachment. Into that silence, the Supreme Court has poured a century of contested decisions, swinging back and forth on how much power the president has to remove agency officials.

The story starts in earnest with **Myers v. United States** in 1926. Chief Justice William Howard Taft, who'd been president himself and knew the frustrations of the office, wrote a sweeping opinion. A law had required Senate consent before the president could remove certain postmasters. The Court struck it down, holding that the president has broad constitutional power to remove executive officers without Senate involvement. The logic was that the president must be able to control the people who carry out the laws, and removal is how that control gets exercised. Myers seemed to establish a strong presidential removal power.

That strong reading lasted less than a decade before the Court carved out a major exception. In **Humphrey's Executor v. United States** in 1935, the Court confronted a president trying to remove an FTC commissioner over policy disagreements. Franklin Roosevelt wanted William Humphrey off the commission because Humphrey's views clashed with the New Deal, and Roosevelt fired him even though the statute allowed removal only for cause. The Court sided against the president. It reasoned that the FTC wasn't a purely executive body; it also did quasi-legislative work (writing rules) and quasi-judicial work (deciding cases). For an agency like that, the Court held, Congress could legitimately protect the commissioners from at-will removal. Humphrey's Executor became the constitutional foundation for the entire independent-agency model. Without it, for-cause removal protection would collapse.

For decades, these two cases coexisted uneasily. Myers gave the president broad removal power over executive officials; Humphrey's Executor let Congress shield the leaders of independent commissions. Where exactly the line fell was never perfectly clear, and later cases kept redrawing it.

In **Morrison v. Olson** in 1988, the Court upheld a law that protected an independent counsel, a prosecutor investigating executive-branch wrongdoing, from at-will removal. The vote was lopsided, seven to one, in favor of the removal restriction. The Court applied a functional test, asking whether the protection stopped the president from carrying out his constitutional duties, and concluded it didn't. The one dissenter was Justice Antonin Scalia, whose solo opinion argued that the president must have complete control over anyone exercising executive power. At the time, Scalia's view was the losing view. Over the following decades, it gained ground, and his dissent is now cited more often than the majority he was writing against.

The Court began tightening the president's control again in the 2000s. In **Free Enterprise Fund v. Public Company Accounting Oversight Board** in 2010, it struck down what it called "double for-cause" protection. The board in question, which oversees the auditing of public companies, was made up of members who could be removed only for cause by the SEC, whose commissioners could themselves be removed only for cause. Two layers of protection stacked on top of each other, and the Court held that was too much. Chief Justice John Roberts wrote that stacking the protections stripped the president of the control the Constitution requires, because the president couldn't reach the board's members even indirectly. The Court fixed the problem by removing one layer, making the board members removable at will by the SEC.

The most recent chapter came in **Seila Law v. Consumer Financial Protection Bureau** in 2020. The CFPB, created after the 2008 financial crisis, was headed by a single director who served a fixed term and could be removed only for cause. The Court struck down that structure. Roberts, writing again, held that concentrating so much power in a single official who was insulated from presidential control violated the separation of powers. He distinguished the earlier cases carefully: Humphrey's Executor covered multimember commissions, and Morrison covered inferior officers, but a single powerful director protected from removal fit neither exception. The Court kept the CFPB alive by severing the removal restriction, making its director removable at will. A year later, in **Collins v. Yellen** in 2021, the Court applied the same reasoning to another single-director agency, the Federal Housing Finance Agency, and struck down its removal protection too.

Here's the arc of the major removal cases.

Case	Year	Question	Result
Myers v. United States	1926	Can Congress require Senate consent to remove an executive officer?	No; broad presidential removal power

Humphrey's Executor	1935	Can Congress protect independent commissioners from at-will removal?	Yes; foundation of independent agencies
Morrison v. Olson	1988	Can an independent counsel be protected from removal?	Yes, 7–1; Scalia's lone dissent
Free Enterprise Fund	2010	Is double for-cause protection allowed?	No; one layer severed
Seila Law v. CFPB	2020	Can a single agency director have for-cause protection?	No; restriction severed
Collins v. Yellen	2021	Same question for the FHFA	No; restriction severed

Read together, these cases show a clear direction over the last two decades. The Court has grown more skeptical of restrictions on the president's removal power and more willing to strike them down. The multimember independent commissions protected by Humphrey's Executor still stand, but the exception has been narrowed, and some observers think Humphrey's Executor itself could eventually be revisited. If that happened, the constitutional footing under every independent agency would shift. For now, the practical takeaway is that the president's control over agency leadership is stronger than it was a generation ago, and the trend has been running in the president's favor.

Organizational Charts and Internal Agency Hierarchy

Step inside any large agency and you find a layered structure, with political appointees at the top and career staff filling out everything below. Understanding this internal arrangement explains a puzzle that confuses a lot of people: how agencies can change direction with each new president while somehow staying more or less consistent year to year. The answer is that agencies run on two different kinds of people, and only one kind turns over with elections.

At the top sit the **political appointees**. These are the secretary or administrator, the deputy, and a layer of under secretaries and assistant secretaries who set policy and direction. They're chosen by the president, they share the administration's goals, and they leave when the administration does. The top ones require Senate confirmation. This layer is thin, usually a few hundred people even in a big department, but it holds the power to set priorities and steer the agency.

Below them sit the **career civil servants**, and this is where most of the agency lives. These are the scientists, lawyers, analysts, inspectors, and administrators who do the actual work. They're hired through a merit-based system, not appointed for political reasons, and they stay through changes in administration. A scientist at the

EPA might serve under presidents of both parties across a thirty-year career. Career staff carry protections against being fired for political reasons, which is meant to keep the government's expert workforce stable and shielded from patronage. The top career managers belong to a group called the Senior Executive Service, which sits just below the political appointees and links the two worlds.

This two-layer design creates a built-in tension that shapes how agencies operate. The political appointees want to change direction quickly to match the president's agenda. The career staff carry institutional knowledge, established ways of doing things, and their own professional judgment about what works.

When a new administration pushes hard for change, the career workforce can act as either a partner or a brake, depending on whether the staff agree with where things are headed. Neither side fully controls the agency alone, and the interaction between them determines how much a new president can actually accomplish.

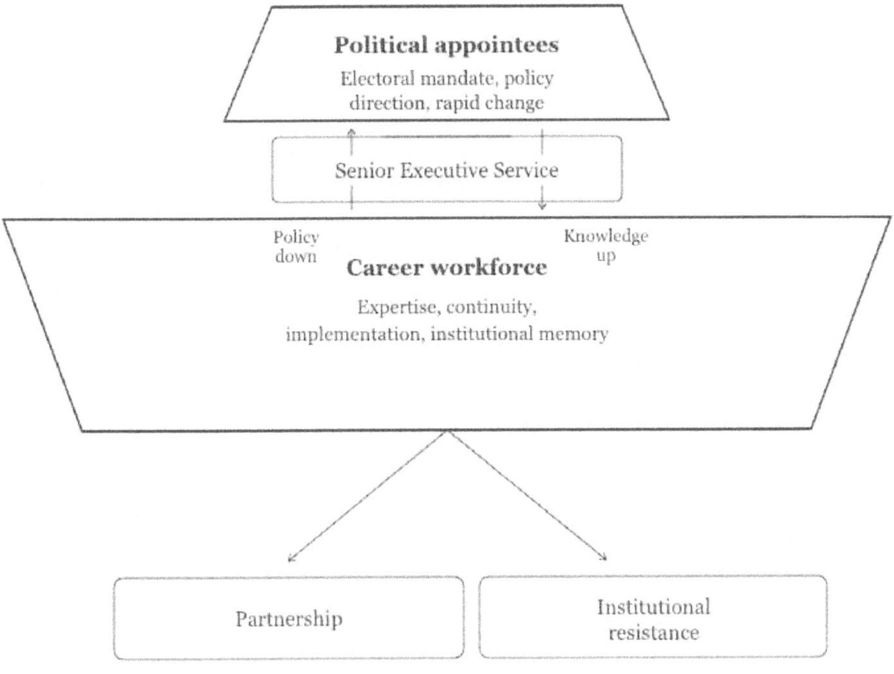

Outcome depends on interaction, not control by either side alone

Here's the basic split.

Layer	Who they are	Selected how	Stay or go

Political appointees	Secretary, deputies, assistant secretaries	Appointed by the president; top ones confirmed by Senate	Leave with the administration
Senior Executive Service	Top career managers	Merit-based, competitive selection	Generally stay
Career civil servants	Scientists, lawyers, analysts, inspectors	Merit-based hiring	Stay across administrations

A few specialized offices appear inside almost every agency, and they're worth knowing because they show up throughout this book. The **general counsel's office** provides the agency's legal advice and defends it in disputes. The **office of inspector general** investigates waste, fraud, and misconduct inside the agency, operating with a degree of independence so it can investigate its own agency honestly. And in agencies that hold hearings, the **administrative law judges** preside over adjudications, deciding individual cases under the agency's rules. Each of these plays a distinct part, and later chapters return to them: inspectors general in the discussion of oversight, and administrative law judges in the discussion of how agencies decide cases.

The regional structure adds one more dimension. Many agencies don't operate only from Washington; they run field offices spread across the country. The EPA has ten regional offices. The IRS, the Social Security Administration, and many others maintain local offices that handle the agency's work on the ground. This matters because the agency you deal with in practice is often a regional office staffed by career employees, far from the political leadership in the capital. The person who inspects a factory or processes a benefits claim is usually a career civil servant in a field office, applying rules set in Washington but exercising real judgment in how they're carried out.

Discussion Question

The Supreme Court has spent a century deciding how much the president can control agency leaders, and lately it's leaned toward giving the president more control by striking down removal protections. Independent agencies were built on the opposite idea, that some decisions, like setting interest rates or policing securities markets, work better when they're insulated from whoever happens to be in office. If the Court eventually removed those protections entirely and made every agency head answerable to the president at will, what would the country gain, what would it lose, and are there some government functions that simply shouldn't bend to electoral politics?

Chapter 3: Sources of Agency Power and Legal Authority

Ask an agency where it gets the power to tell you what to do, and there's always an answer. It might be buried in a statute passed decades ago, or spelled out in a presidential order, or implied by the nature of a job Congress assigned. But the answer exists, and it has to, because no agency in the United States can act on its own say-so. Every rule, every fine, every permit denial traces back to a grant of authority from somewhere. Pull that thread and it leads, sooner or later, to Congress or the Constitution.

This is the single most important thing to understand about agency power: agencies are creatures of statute. They don't exist until a law creates them, and they can't do anything a law hasn't authorized. A private company can do whatever isn't forbidden. An agency is the reverse. It can do only what it's been permitted to do, and everything else is off-limits. When an agency acts beyond its granted authority, courts describe the action with a Latin phrase, ultra vires, meaning beyond the powers, and they can wipe it out.

That principle sounds abstract until you watch it stop a real agency in its tracks. This chapter works through the sources agencies draw on: the statutes that create them and hand them power, the master procedural law that governs how they use it, the presidential orders that direct them, the mandates that tell them what they must accomplish, and finally the question of whether agencies have any power that doesn't come from a grant at all. By the end, you'll be able to look at any agency action and ask the right first question: who said you could?

Enabling Statutes and Congressional Delegation

Every agency is born from a law. That law, called the **enabling statute** (sometimes the organic statute or organic act), is the document that creates the agency, defines its mission, and hands it the powers it needs to do its job. If you want to know what an agency can and can't do, the enabling statute is where you start. It's the agency's charter, its instruction manual, and the outer boundary of its authority all at once.

Think of the enabling statute as the source code. The Environmental Protection Agency draws its power from a set of statutes including the Clean Air Act and the Clean Water Act. The Securities and Exchange Commission operates under the Securities Act of 1933 and the Securities Exchange Act of 1934. The Occupational Safety and Health Administration works under the Occupational Safety and Health Act of 1970. Each of these laws tells its agency what subject it governs, what tools it has, and what goals it's supposed to pursue. Take the statute away and the agency has nothing.

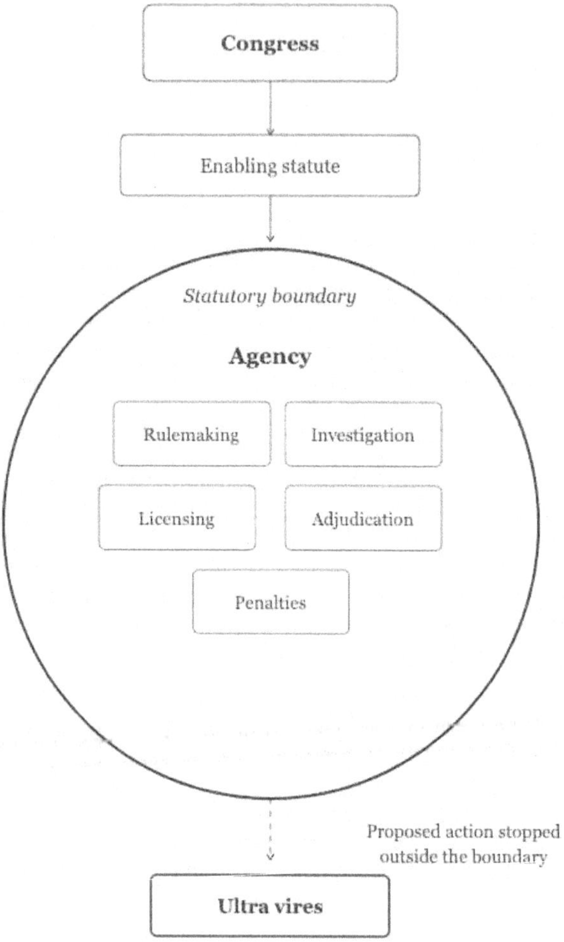

Here's a sampling of major agencies and the statutes that empower them.

Agency	Enabling Statute(s)	Subject Granted
EPA	Clean Air Act, Clean Water Act	Air and water pollution
SEC	Securities Act of 1933, Securities Exchange Act of 1934	Securities markets
OSHA	Occupational Safety and Health Act of 1970	Workplace safety
FCC	Communications Act of 1934	Broadcasting, telecommunications

FTC	Federal Trade Commission Act of 1914	Unfair business practices
FDA	Federal Food, Drug, and Cosmetic Act of 1938	Food, drugs, medical devices
NLRB	National Labor Relations Act of 1935	Union organizing, collective bargaining

What an enabling statute contains. These statutes typically do several things. They establish the agency as a legal body. They define its jurisdiction, meaning the subject matter it's allowed to regulate. They grant specific powers, like the power to issue rules, hold hearings, conduct investigations, and impose penalties. And they set out the goals the agency should pursue, sometimes in precise terms and sometimes in broad ones. The mix of specific and broad language in an enabling statute determines how much room the agency has to maneuver, and it's often where legal fights begin.

The breadth of the grant varies enormously from statute to statute. Some enabling statutes are narrow, giving an agency a tightly defined task with little discretion. Others are sweeping, handing the agency a broad goal and trusting it to work out the details. The Clean Air Act tells the EPA to set air quality standards "requisite to protect the public health," which leaves the agency wide latitude to decide what that means. A narrower statute might specify exact numbers, deadlines, and procedures, leaving the agency little to figure out. Reading an enabling statute carefully, and noticing whether its language is tight or loose, is the first skill of anyone trying to predict what an agency can get away with.

When an agency reaches too far. The limits built into enabling statutes aren't theoretical. Courts enforce them, and sometimes they stop agencies from doing things that might otherwise seem sensible. The clearest illustration is the long fight over whether the FDA could regulate tobacco.

In the 1990s, the FDA decided that cigarettes, as products that deliver the drug nicotine, fell under its authority to regulate drugs and devices. The agency issued rules restricting the sale and marketing of tobacco to young people. The tobacco industry sued, arguing that the FDA's enabling statute, the Food, Drug, and Cosmetic Act, didn't actually give the agency power over tobacco. The case reached the Supreme Court, and in **FDA v. Brown & Williamson Tobacco Corp.** in 2000, the Court sided with the industry. It held that the FDA had overstepped its statutory authority.

The reasoning matters, because it wasn't about whether regulating tobacco was wise. The Court looked at the whole history of tobacco legislation and concluded that Congress had repeatedly addressed tobacco through separate, specific laws while deliberately keeping it out of the FDA's hands. Reading the FDA's statute to cover tobacco would have clashed with everything Congress had done on the subject. If the FDA's reading were right, the Court noted, the agency would have to ban cigarettes outright as unsafe, which Congress plainly never intended. So the FDA lost, not because its policy was bad, but because its enabling statute didn't stretch that far.

The story has a revealing sequel. When an agency lacks power under its enabling statute, the fix is for Congress to grant the power. That's exactly what happened. In 2009, Congress passed the Family Smoking Prevention and Tobacco Control Act, which explicitly gave the FDA authority over tobacco products. The same regulation the courts had blocked in 2000 became lawful once Congress supplied the missing authority. The episode shows the whole system in motion: an agency can only act within its granted powers, and if the powers aren't there, only Congress can add them.

Delegation as a two-way relationship. Congressional delegation, the act of handing power to an agency, is really a relationship that continues over time. Congress doesn't just create an agency and walk away. It amends enabling statutes, adds new duties, takes away others, and adjusts the agency's authority as circumstances change. The Clean Air Act has been amended several times, each round expanding or refining the EPA's powers. So an agency's authority isn't fixed at birth; it evolves as Congress revisits the enabling statute.

This ongoing relationship is why the exact words of a statute carry so much weight in administrative law. When a dispute arises over whether an agency can do something, the argument almost always turns on what the enabling statute says and what Congress meant by it. Lawyers parse individual words, trace the statute's history, and compare it to related laws. The outcome often hinges on whether a particular grant of power was broad enough to cover what the agency did. This is the daily work of the field, and it all flows from the basic principle that the statute is the source and the limit of everything the agency can do.

The Administrative Procedure Act of 1946

If enabling statutes tell each agency what it can do, one law tells nearly all of them how they must do it. The **Administrative Procedure Act of 1946**, usually just called the APA, is the master statute of federal administrative law. It sets the ground rules for how agencies make regulations, how they decide cases, and how courts review their work. People sometimes call it the constitution of administrative law, and the description fits, because almost everything in the field runs through it.

The APA came out of a real problem. By the 1940s, agencies had multiplied so fast, especially during the New Deal, that the process itself was chaotic. Each agency followed its own procedures. There were no consistent rules about how an agency had to write a regulation, what notice it had to give the public, or how it had to run a hearing. Businesses complained they were being treated arbitrarily, with no way to predict or challenge what agencies did. Reformers worried the whole system lacked fairness and accountability. Something had to bring order to it.

The road to the APA was contentious. An earlier attempt, the Walter-Logan Act, passed Congress in 1940, but President Roosevelt vetoed it, seeing it as an effort to hobble his agencies. A more careful process followed. The Attorney General assembled a committee to study administrative procedure, and its detailed 1941 report laid the groundwork. After years of negotiation between people who wanted stronger agencies and people who wanted tighter controls, Congress reached a compromise everyone could accept, and President Truman signed the APA into law in 1946. Its passage without serious opposition reflected how badly the system needed a common set of rules.

What the APA actually does. The genius of the APA is that it created uniform procedures that apply across the entire federal government, no matter which agency is acting. It sorts nearly everything agencies do into two broad categories, the same two introduced earlier in this book: rulemaking, where an agency writes a regulation that applies broadly, and adjudication, where an agency decides a specific case. For each category, the APA sets out procedures, and it distinguishes between formal proceedings, which require trial-like hearings, and informal ones, which don't.

The statute is organized into sections, and a handful of them do most of the work. Knowing what these sections cover gives you a map of the whole field.

APA Section	What It Governs
551	Definitions (rule, order, agency, adjudication, and more)
553	Rulemaking, including notice-and-comment procedures
554	Formal adjudication requirements
556 and 557	Procedures for formal hearings, evidence, and decisions
555	General procedural rights, including the right to counsel
702	The right to judicial review of agency action
706	The scope of judicial review and the standards courts apply

Section 553 is the heart of federal rulemaking. It lays out the process an agency generally must follow to issue a regulation: publish a notice of the proposed rule, let the public submit comments, consider those comments, and then publish the final rule with an explanation. This procedure, known as notice-and-comment rulemaking, is how most federal regulations get made, and the next chapter covers it in full detail. For now, the point is that the requirement lives in the APA, and it applies to agencies across the government unless a more specific statute says otherwise.

Section 706 is the other giant. It tells courts how to review agency action and what standards to use. Among other things, it directs courts to set aside agency actions that are "arbitrary, capricious, an abuse of discretion, or otherwise not in accordance with law." That phrase, "arbitrary and capricious," has become one of the most litigated standards in all of administrative law, and Chapter 6 unpacks what it means. Section 706 also provides the "substantial evidence" standard that applies to certain formal proceedings. These standards determine how much deference courts give agencies and how easily a person can get an agency decision overturned.

How the APA fits with other statutes. A common source of confusion is how the APA relates to each agency's own enabling statute, so it's worth being clear. The APA provides the default rules. It applies to every federal agency and every action unless a more specific statute overrides it. Many enabling statutes add their own procedural requirements on top of the APA, and when they do, those specific requirements govern. So an agency's procedure is often a blend: the APA's baseline, plus whatever extra steps its own statute demands.

This layering means you can't understand an agency's procedures by reading the APA alone, or by reading the enabling statute alone. You have to read them together. The enabling statute might require the agency to hold additional hearings, consider particular factors, or meet specific deadlines that the APA doesn't mention. Where the enabling statute is silent, the APA fills the gap. Where it speaks, it usually controls. Keeping this relationship straight saves a lot of confusion, because a question about "what procedure applies" almost always requires checking both laws.

The APA's deliberate gaps. One surprising thing about the APA is how skeletal it is. For a statute this important, it's remarkably brief and leaves a lot unsaid. It sets out basic procedures but doesn't spell out many of the details that turn out to matter most. What exactly does an agency have to include in a notice of proposed rulemaking? How thoroughly must it respond to public comments? When is an agency's explanation good enough to survive review? The APA doesn't answer these questions directly.

Courts filled in the blanks. Over the decades since 1946, judges have built an enormous body of case law interpreting the APA, adding requirements the text doesn't literally state. The demand that agencies respond to significant public comments, for instance, isn't spelled out in the statute; courts read it in. The requirement that an agency give a reasoned explanation for its choices grew the same way. So the APA as it operates today is really the statute plus seventy-plus years of judicial interpretation layered on top. This is why administrative law can't be learned from the statute book alone, and why so much of this field lives in court decisions rather than in the words Congress wrote.

Executive Orders and Presidential Directives

Congress isn't the only source of direction for agencies. The president also steers them, mainly through **executive orders** and other presidential directives. An executive order is a written command from the president to the executive branch, and when it rests on legitimate authority, it carries the force of law within the government. Presidents use these orders to set policy, direct agencies to act, and manage how the executive branch operates.

It's important to be clear about what an executive order is and isn't. It's not a law passed by Congress. The president can't create a statute by executive order, and can't order agencies to do things Congress has forbidden. An executive order is only as strong as the authority behind it. That authority comes from one of two places: a power the Constitution gives the president directly, or a power Congress has delegated by statute. When an executive order rests on solid constitutional or statutory ground, it binds the executive branch and can reshape how agencies work. When it reaches beyond that ground, courts can strike it down.

The framework for presidential power. The definitive statement of how far presidential authority extends comes from a 1952 case that's become one of the most cited decisions in American law. During the Korean War, President Truman feared a steelworkers' strike would cripple production, so he issued an executive order seizing the nation's steel mills to keep them running. The steel companies sued, and in **Youngstown Sheet & Tube Co. v. Sawyer**, the Supreme Court ruled against the president. Truman had no statute authorizing the seizure, and the Court found he lacked the constitutional power to take private property this way on his own.

The lasting contribution of Youngstown wasn't the majority opinion but a concurrence by Justice Robert Jackson, which laid out a three-part framework for judging presidential power that courts still use today. Jackson's insight was that presidential authority isn't fixed; it rises and falls depending on whether the president is acting with or against Congress.

Situation	Presidential Power	Explanation
President acts with congressional authorization	Highest	Power combines the president's own authority plus what Congress grants
Congress is silent (the "zone of twilight")	Uncertain	President relies on independent authority; legality depends on circumstances
President acts against Congress's will	Lowest	Power is at its "lowest ebb"; the president must rely on constitutional authority alone

This framework governs how courts evaluate executive orders and other presidential actions. An order that carries out a power Congress has granted stands on the strongest footing. An order that contradicts what Congress has decided stands on the weakest. Truman's steel seizure fell into that weakest category, because Congress had considered giving presidents seizure power and declined, so the Court struck it down. Jackson's three tiers turned a single wartime dispute into a lasting tool for measuring the limits of presidential authority.

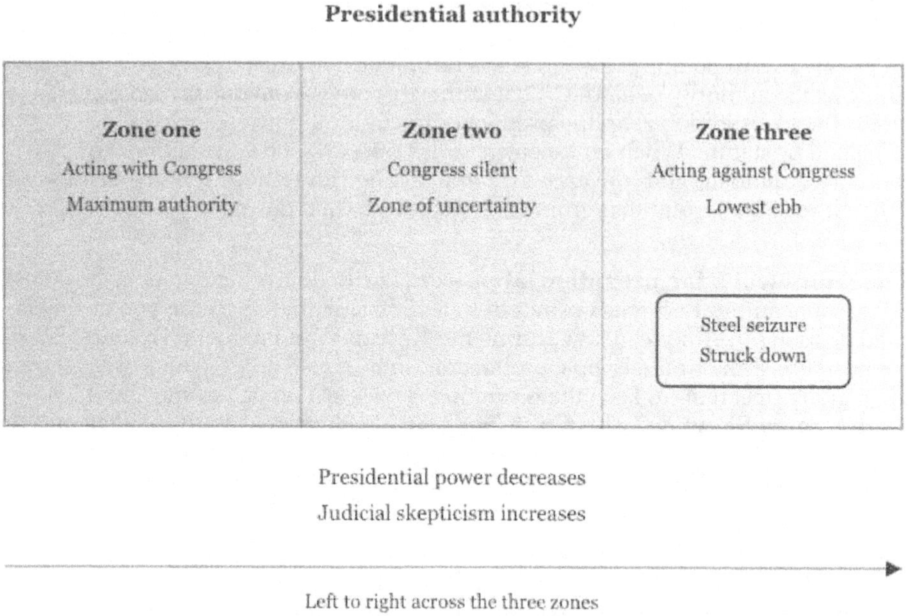

Executive orders that shape administrative law. Some executive orders have become permanent parts of how agencies operate, outlasting the presidents who issued them. The most consequential for this field concern how agencies review their own regulations before issuing them.

In 1993, President Clinton issued Executive Order 12866, which set up a system of centralized review for major regulations. Under it, agencies must analyze the costs and benefits of their significant rules and submit them to an office inside the White House, the Office of Information and Regulatory Affairs (OIRA), for review before the rules take effect. This order, which built on an earlier one from the Reagan administration, gives the president a check on what agencies produce. If OIRA raises concerns about a rule's costs, the agency has to address them before moving forward. Executive Order 12866 has remained in force across administrations of both parties, becoming a fixture of the rulemaking process, and it's a good example of how a presidential directive can shape administrative practice for decades.

Presidents also use other kinds of directives beyond formal executive orders. Presidential memoranda work much like executive orders but with fewer formal requirements. Proclamations announce policy, often on ceremonial or trade matters. Signing statements, issued when the president signs a bill, express the president's interpretation of the new law and can guide how agencies carry it out. All of these are ways the president directs the executive branch without going through Congress, and all of them face the same basic limit: they're valid only to the extent they rest on real authority. A directive that oversteps the president's power is subject to challenge in court, just as an executive order is.

Agency Charters and Statutory Mandates

An enabling statute doesn't only grant power; it also imposes duties. The mission an agency is directed to accomplish, its **statutory mandate**, is the set of marching orders that tells the agency not just what it may do but what it must do. Understanding mandates matters because they constrain agency discretion from the other direction. Where a grant of power says the agency is allowed to act, a mandate says the agency is required to act, and the difference has real legal consequences.

The clue often lies in a single word. Statutes that say an agency "shall" do something impose a mandatory duty, while statutes that say an agency "may" do something grant discretion. When Congress writes that the EPA "shall" set a standard for a pollutant, it's issuing a command, not an option. When it writes that an agency "may" issue rules on a subject, it's leaving the choice to the agency. Courts take this distinction seriously. An agency that ignores a mandatory duty can be sued and ordered to perform it, while an agency exercising genuine discretion has far more freedom.

When a mandate forces an agency to act. The power of a statutory mandate shows clearly in the fight over greenhouse gases. For years, the EPA declined to regulate the emissions from cars that contribute to climate change, arguing that it either lacked authority or shouldn't exercise it. A group of states and organizations sued, pointing to the Clean Air Act's language directing the EPA to regulate air pollutants that endanger public health. The case reached the Supreme Court, and in **Massachusetts v. EPA** in 2007, the Court held that greenhouse gases are air pollutants under the statute and that the EPA couldn't simply refuse to decide whether they endanger public health.

The ruling didn't force the EPA to adopt any particular rule. What it did was strip away the agency's claim that it could just walk away from the question. The statute gave the EPA a duty to make a judgment based on the science, and the Court held the agency to it. The EPA had to either find that greenhouse gases endanger public health and welfare or explain, on scientific grounds, why they don't. The agency couldn't dodge the decision on grounds the statute didn't allow. This is what a mandate does: it converts a subject the agency might prefer to avoid into a duty the agency has to confront.

Deadlines and the problem of competing commands. Many statutory mandates come with deadlines, and Congress sometimes uses them to force agencies to move. Environmental laws in particular are full of deadlines requiring the agency to issue standards by certain dates, a technique meant to prevent agencies from stalling forever. When an agency misses a mandatory deadline, citizens or organizations can often sue to compel action, using provisions in the statute that let private parties enforce the agency's duties. These deadlines don't always work, because agencies miss them routinely and courts can only push so hard, but they represent Congress's attempt to keep agencies from sitting on their hands.

Mandates also create a harder problem when they conflict. Agencies frequently operate under multiple directives that pull in different directions. An agency might be told to protect public health, but also to consider the economic costs of its rules, and also to act by a certain deadline. These commands can't always be satisfied at once. Protecting health to the maximum might cost too much; meeting the deadline might mean cutting corners on the analysis. When mandates collide, the agency has to balance them, and courts reviewing the result have to decide whether the agency struck a reasonable balance or ignored one of its duties. Much of the difficulty in running an agency comes from serving several masters at the same time, each represented by a different clause in the enabling statute.

Inherent vs. Delegated Authority

The chapter closes with a distinction that ties everything together. All the sources of power discussed so far, enabling statutes, mandates, even executive orders resting on delegated authority, share one feature: they're grants. Someone with authority hands power to the agency. This is **delegated authority**, and it's the foundation of nearly everything agencies do. But it raises a question worth answering directly: do agencies have any power that doesn't come from a grant? Do they possess **inherent authority**, power that belongs to them simply because of what they are?

The general answer is no, and this is one of the firmest rules in the field. Agencies have no inherent authority. Because they're creatures of statute, created by law and defined by law, they possess only the powers Congress gives them. An agency can't reach into some reservoir of inherent power to justify an action Congress never authorized. If the authority isn't in the statute, expressly or by fair implication, the agency doesn't have it. This is what makes agencies fundamentally different from some other actors in government.

The contrast with the president sharpens the point. The president can plausibly claim certain inherent powers that flow directly from the Constitution, from the grant of "executive Power" in Article II. Presidents have long argued they hold authority in areas like foreign affairs and national security that doesn't depend on any statute. Whether and how far these inherent presidential powers extend is itself contested, as Youngstown showed, but the claim is at least available to the president. It isn't available to agencies. An agency has no constitutional grant of its own to draw on. It has only what Congress delegated.

Implied powers, which are still delegated. There's an important refinement here that people sometimes mistake for inherent authority. Agencies do have **implied powers**, meaning powers reasonably necessary to carry out the express powers Congress granted. If a statute gives an agency the power to regulate an industry but doesn't spell out every tool needed to do it, courts will usually find that the agency has the implied authority to take steps reasonably necessary to accomplish the assigned task. An agency told to enforce a law can generally issue subpoenas to gather evidence, even if the statute doesn't say so in exact words, because that power is fairly implied by the enforcement duty.

But implied authority isn't inherent authority, and the difference matters. Implied powers still trace back to a delegation. They're powers reasonably necessary to execute what Congress expressly granted, so they flow from the statute, just less directly. Inherent authority, by contrast, would mean power that exists independent of any grant. Agencies have the first and not the second. The line can get blurry in hard cases, where the question is whether a particular power is fairly implied by the statute or reaches beyond it, and courts sometimes disagree. But the framework is clear: an agency's power, whether express or implied, must connect back to something Congress delegated.

Here's the distinction laid out.

Type of Authority	Source	Do Agencies Have It?
Delegated (express)	Explicitly granted by statute	Yes, this is the core of agency power
Implied	Reasonably necessary to carry out express powers	Yes, but still traces to the statute
Inherent	Belongs to the body by its nature, no grant needed	No, agencies possess only what's delegated

This principle has practical bite. When an agency claims a power, the question is always whether that power can be traced to a statutory grant, directly or by fair implication. An agency can't defend an action by saying it has always done things this way, or that the action is a reasonable thing for a government body to do. It has to point to the statute. This is why so many administrative law disputes come down to reading the enabling statute closely and asking whether the agency's claimed power really lives there. If it does, the agency wins. If it doesn't, no amount of good intentions or practical sense will supply the missing authority, because agencies simply don't have any power to give themselves.

Discussion Question

Agencies can't act without a grant of authority from Congress, yet Congress often writes enabling statutes in broad, open language and lets agencies work out what the words mean in practice, sometimes stretching an old statute to cover problems its authors never imagined, like the EPA reading a 1970 clean-air law to reach greenhouse gases. When does an agency's interpretation of a vague grant count as faithfully carrying out what Congress delegated, and when does it become the agency quietly handing itself power Congress never actually gave? Is there a workable way to tell the difference, or does it always come down to whether a judge happens to like the result?

Chapter 4: Rulemaking Procedures

There's a government website where anyone can go to argue with a federal agency, and millions of people do. It's called regulations.gov, and on any given day it holds proposed rules on everything from truck emissions to the sugar content of school lunches, each one open for public comment. A cattle rancher in Nebraska, a lawyer at a Fortune 500 company, and a college student with an opinion all get the same box to type into. The agency has to read what they write.

That setup captures something surprising about how American law actually gets made. Most of the binding rules people live under weren't voted on by anyone. They came out of a process where an agency proposed something, the public responded, and the agency finalized a version that carries the force of law. This process is called rulemaking, and it's the closest thing agencies have to a legislative power. This chapter takes apart how it works, starting with the version that produces the overwhelming majority of federal regulations.

Notice-and-Comment Rulemaking

The standard way agencies make rules goes by the name **notice-and-comment rulemaking**, and it's built on a simple democratic idea: before the government imposes a rule on you, it should tell you what it plans to do and let you have your say. The process comes from Section 553 of the Administrative Procedure Act, and while the statute describes it in a few short paragraphs, the reality has grown into something far more involved. Understanding the three basic steps, and how much heavier each has become over time, tells you most of what you need to know about how regulations are born.

Step one: the proposal. Everything starts when an agency publishes a **Notice of Proposed Rulemaking**, usually called an NPRM, in the Federal Register. The Federal Register is the government's official daily newspaper, the place where agencies announce what they're doing.

The notice has to tell the public several things – that the agency is proposing a rule, what legal authority it's acting under, and what the proposed rule actually says or describes. In practice, agencies publish the full text of the rule they have in mind, along with a lengthy explanation of the problem they're trying to solve and the reasoning behind their approach.

This proposal stage does more work than it might seem. The notice sets the terms of the entire proceeding. It tells the public what's on the table, and, as you'll see, it limits how far the final rule can stray from what was proposed. An agency that wants to regulate has to commit, in writing and in public, to a specific plan before anyone weighs in.

Step two: the comment period. Once the proposal is published, the agency opens a window for the public to respond. This comment period typically runs 30 to

60 days, though agencies can make it longer for complicated rules, and sometimes extend it under pressure. During this window, anyone can submit written comments: individuals, businesses, trade associations, advocacy groups, other government bodies, and experts of every kind. The comments arrive through regulations.gov, and for major rules they can number in the hundreds of thousands or even the millions.

Not all comments carry the same weight, and it helps to understand why. A form letter submitted a million times by an organized campaign counts as public sentiment, but it doesn't do much legally. What matters most are substantive comments that raise real problems: technical flaws in the agency's data, legal objections, unintended consequences the agency missed, or better alternatives. A single well-researched comment from an industry expert or a scientist can reshape a rule far more than a flood of identical postcards. The comment period isn't a vote, and the agency isn't required to do what the majority wants. It's a chance to give the agency information and arguments it has to grapple with.

Step three: the final rule. After the comment period closes, the agency reviews what came in and decides how to proceed. It might finalize the rule as proposed, change it in response to the comments, or occasionally withdraw it altogether. When it issues the final rule, the APA requires the agency to include what the statute calls a "concise general statement of their basis and purpose." That sounds modest, and Congress probably meant it to be. It hasn't stayed modest.

Courts have transformed that short phrase into a demanding requirement. A "concise general statement" today often runs to hundreds of pages, because courts have held that agencies must respond to all the significant comments they received. If a commenter raised a serious objection, the agency can't just ignore it; it has to address the point and explain why it went the way it did. If the agency changed course based on a comment, it has to say so and explain the change. This duty to respond, which appears nowhere in the literal text of the APA, is now one of the central obligations of rulemaking, and it's a big reason final rules come wrapped in enormous explanatory preambles. An agency that brushes past a serious comment risks having its rule struck down as arbitrary and capricious.

Here's the basic sequence.

Step	What Happens	Where
Notice	Agency publishes proposed rule with its reasoning and legal basis	Federal Register
Comment	Public submits written responses, typically over 30–60 days	Regulations.gov
Final rule	Agency responds to significant comments and issues the final version	Federal Register

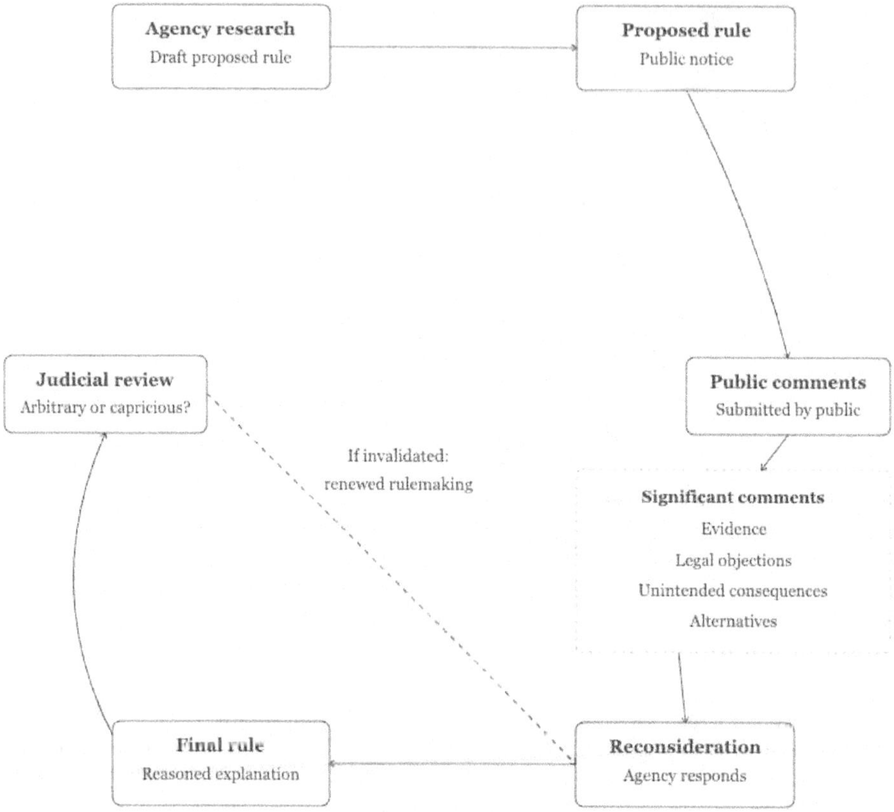

The logical outgrowth rule. One constraint ties the proposal to the final product. The final rule has to be a "logical outgrowth" of the proposed rule. This means the agency can change the rule in response to comments, but it can't spring something entirely new that the public never had a chance to address. The test is whether interested parties should reasonably have anticipated that the final rule might look the way it does, based on the proposal. If the agency's final rule veers off in a direction nobody could have seen coming, courts will say the agency failed to give proper notice, and the agency has to propose the new version and take comments all over again. This rule keeps the notice meaningful. An agency can't propose one thing, collect comments, and then quietly finalize something completely different.

Legislative rules versus guidance. Not everything an agency writes goes through this process, and the exceptions cause a lot of fighting. Notice-and-comment procedures apply to **legislative rules**, also called substantive rules, which are the ones that carry the force of law and create new legal obligations. But the APA exempts several other categories from notice and comment: interpretive rules, which explain what an existing rule or statute means; general statements of policy, which announce how an agency intends to exercise its discretion; and rules about the agency's own organization and procedure.

The exemption creates a temptation. Notice-and-comment rulemaking is slow and burdensome, so agencies sometimes try to accomplish their goals by issuing "guidance documents" that they label as interpretive rules or policy statements, skipping the whole comment process. The trouble is that guidance can end up functioning like a binding rule in practice, telling regulated parties what they must do while dodging the procedural protections that a real rule would require. Courts have struggled for years to police the line between genuine guidance, which is exempt, and disguised legislative rules, which aren't. The distinction turns on whether the document actually binds anyone or merely advises them, and it's one of the murkier corners of the field. The Supreme Court weighed in during Perez v. Mortgage Bankers Association in 2015, confirming that agencies can issue and revise interpretive rules without notice and comment, which gave agencies real freedom in this space but left the harder question of when guidance crosses into binding territory unresolved.

Courts can't add procedures. A natural instinct, when a rule affects millions of people, is to think the agency should have to do more: hold hearings, allow cross-examination, gather more evidence. For a while, some lower courts acted on that instinct and imposed extra procedural requirements on agencies beyond what the APA demanded. The Supreme Court shut this down firmly in **Vermont Yankee Nuclear Power Corp. v. Natural Resources Defense Council** in 1978. The Court held that courts can't require agencies to follow procedures beyond those the APA and the agency's own statute impose. If the APA says notice and comment is enough, then notice and comment is enough, and a reviewing court can't demand more just because it would prefer a more elaborate process. Agencies are free to add procedures voluntarily, but courts can't force them to. Vermont Yankee set a boundary that still holds: the procedural floor is what the statute says, and judges don't get to raise it.

Why it all takes so long. Put these requirements together and you can see why making a major rule now takes years, sometimes many years. The agency has to develop the proposal, publish it, run the comment period, read and respond to every significant comment, build a record that will survive court review, and often run the rule through White House review and cost-benefit analysis on top of everything else. Each added requirement, whether from courts, from Congress, or from executive orders, has made the process heavier. Scholars call this problem "ossification," the idea that rulemaking has become so slow and costly that agencies avoid it when they can, reaching for guidance documents or other shortcuts instead. The democratic promise of notice and comment, that the public gets a real say before the government acts, has come at the price of a process so cumbersome that agencies increasingly look for ways around it. That tension, between thoroughness and speed, runs through everything about modern rulemaking.

Formal vs. Informal Rulemaking

Everything described so far is technically the *informal* version of rulemaking, and the name is a little misleading, because there's nothing casual about a process that takes years and generates thousands of pages. It's called informal only in contrast to a more elaborate procedure the APA also provides: **formal rulemaking**. The difference between the two is dramatic, and the story of how formal rulemaking nearly disappeared is one of the more instructive tales in administrative law.

Informal rulemaking is the notice-and-comment process, governed by Section 553. It's paper-based. The public submits written comments, the agency responds in writing, and there's no live hearing, no witnesses, and no cross-examination. This is how the vast majority of federal rules get made.

Formal rulemaking works like a trial. Governed by Sections 556 and 557 of the APA, it requires the agency to hold a full evidentiary hearing, presided over by an administrative law judge, with witnesses who testify under oath, cross-examination, and a decision based on a formal record. It's the difference between mailing in your written thoughts and sitting through a courtroom proceeding that can stretch on for months or years.

When does an agency have to use the formal version? Only when its enabling statute requires that rules be made, in the APA's phrasing, "on the record after opportunity for an agency hearing." Those specific words are the trigger. And here's where the Supreme Court made a decisive move. In **United States v. Florida East Coast Railway** in 1973, the Court held that formal rulemaking is required only when a statute uses language clearly demanding an on-the-record hearing. Absent those magic words, informal rulemaking is enough. Because Congress rarely writes statutes with that exact language, and courts read the requirement narrowly, formal rulemaking became a rarity almost overnight.

There's a good reason courts pushed agencies away from formal rulemaking, and it has a name that administrative law professors love: the peanut butter hearings. In the 1960s and early 1970s, the FDA wanted to set a standard for how much peanut content a product needed before it could be called "peanut butter." The question was whether the minimum should be 90 percent peanuts or 87.5 percent. Because the relevant procedure was formal, the agency had to hold a full trial-type hearing. It dragged on for years. The transcript ran to something like 8,000 pages. Witnesses testified and faced cross-examination over a two-and-a-half-percent difference in peanut content. The proceeding became the standard example of how formal rulemaking could turn a simple regulatory question into an endless, resource-draining ordeal.

That experience convinced nearly everyone that formal rulemaking was a poor fit for setting broad rules. Trial procedures make sense when you're resolving a dispute about specific facts between specific parties. They make far less sense when you're setting a general policy that will apply to a whole industry, where the questions are more about judgment and prediction than about who did what. So formal rulemaking withered, and today it's almost never used.

Here's the contrast.

Feature	Informal Rulemaking	Formal Rulemaking
APA sections	553	553 plus 556 and 557

Process	Written notice and comment	Trial-type evidentiary hearing
Live testimony	No	Yes, under oath
Cross-examination	No	Yes
Presiding officer	None required	Administrative law judge
Trigger	The default	Statute requires decision "on the record after a hearing"
How common	The overwhelming majority of rules	Nearly extinct

Between these two poles sits a middle option that Congress sometimes creates by statute, called **hybrid rulemaking**. In certain areas, Congress has written enabling statutes that require agencies to do more than basic notice and comment but less than a full formal hearing, adding specific procedures like limited oral hearings or additional data requirements. These hybrid procedures don't come from the APA; they come from the individual statute, which is why they vary from agency to agency. They represent Congress's attempt to strike a balance in fields where lawmakers wanted extra process without imposing the full weight of a trial. But hybrid rulemaking exists only where a specific statute creates it, and after Vermont Yankee, courts can't manufacture hybrid procedures on their own.

Interim Final Rules and Emergency Rulemaking

The whole notice-and-comment process assumes there's time to spare, and usually there is. But sometimes there isn't. A disease outbreak, a financial collapse, or a sudden safety hazard can demand a rule immediately, and a process that takes months or years is useless in a genuine emergency. The APA anticipated this, and it provides an escape hatch.

The escape hatch is the **good cause exemption**, found in Section 553. It allows an agency to skip notice and comment when following those procedures would be, in the statute's words, "impracticable, unnecessary, or contrary to the public interest." Each of those three grounds covers a different situation. "Impracticable" applies when there's no time, like an urgent safety threat. "Unnecessary" applies to minor or technical rules where public comment wouldn't add anything, such as correcting a typo in an existing regulation. "Contrary to the public interest" applies when advance notice would defeat the purpose of the rule, for instance if announcing a coming price control would trigger the very hoarding it's meant to prevent.

When an agency uses good cause to skip the normal process, it often issues what's called an **interim final rule**. This is a rule that takes effect immediately, without prior notice and comment, but the agency accepts comments afterward and may revise the rule in response. It's a way of acting fast while still giving the public a delayed say.

A related device, the **direct final rule**, is used for genuinely uncontroversial rules the agency expects no objection to; it takes effect automatically unless someone files an adverse comment, in which case the agency withdraws it and uses the normal process.

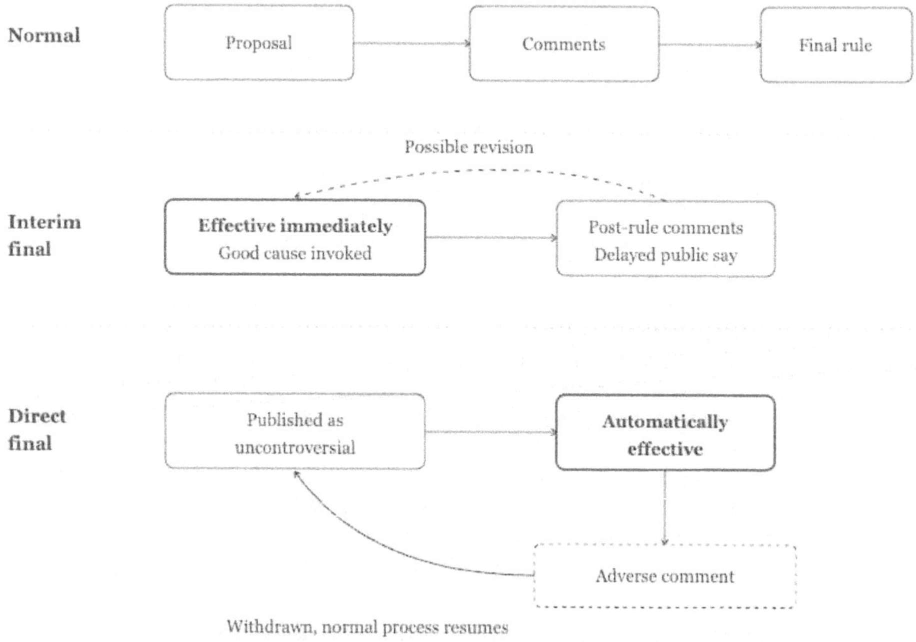

The COVID-19 pandemic in 2020 produced a wave of these emergency rules. Agencies across the government issued interim final rules to respond to the crisis, waiving normal requirements, adjusting healthcare rules, and changing how programs operated, all on the strength of the good cause exemption. The pandemic was close to a textbook case for the exemption, because waiting months for a comment period while a public health emergency unfolded would have been genuinely impracticable.

Courts don't let agencies stretch this exemption freely, and that's the part agencies most often forget. The good cause exemption is read narrowly, and courts have struck down rules where agencies claimed emergency justification that didn't hold up. An agency can't invoke good cause just because notice and comment is inconvenient or because it's in a hurry for reasons of its own making. The emergency has to be real, and the agency has to explain why the situation genuinely made normal procedures impracticable. When agencies try to use the exemption as a shortcut around a process they'd simply rather avoid, courts have shown they're willing to invalidate the resulting rules. The exemption is a safety valve for true emergencies, not a general license to skip the public's role.

Discussion Question

Notice-and-comment rulemaking was designed to give ordinary people a voice in the rules that govern them, but the process has grown so slow and demanding that agencies now dodge it whenever they can, issuing "guidance" that binds in practice while skipping the comment period entirely.

Did the courts, by piling on requirements to make rulemaking more thorough, end up making the public's voice weaker rather than stronger? And if a faster, lighter process would mean agencies actually used it, would that be a better deal for the people it's supposed to protect?

Chapter 5: Adjudication and Enforcement

Walk into the headquarters of the Securities and Exchange Commission and you'll find something that looks a lot like a courtroom. There's a bench, a witness stand, tables for the lawyers, and a judge who runs the proceedings. Testimony gets taken, evidence gets weighed, and someone walks out having won or lost. The one thing missing is the thing most people associate with American justice: it isn't part of the judicial branch at all. The judge works for the SEC. The prosecutor works for the SEC. The rules come from the SEC. And until recently, if the agency accused you of securities fraud, this was often the room where your case would be decided, with no jury anywhere in sight.

That arrangement, an agency running its own courts, is one of the stranger features of American government, and it's under more pressure right now than it has been in decades. In 2024, the Supreme Court looked at the SEC's in-house courts and said that for certain cases, the whole setup violates the Constitution. We'll get to that decision, because it may reshape how agencies enforce the law for years to come.

This chapter is about what agencies do when they stop writing rules and start applying them to specific people and businesses. Rulemaking, the subject of the last chapter, is how agencies make law that applies to everyone. Adjudication and enforcement are how agencies act against particular parties: deciding individual cases, imposing penalties, granting and revoking licenses, and investigating suspected wrongdoing. This is where agency power stops being abstract and lands on a specific company, a specific professional, a specific permit. It's also where the constitutional protections people expect from the legal system get tested, because agencies exercise power that looks judicial without being courts.

Formal Adjudication Hearings

Adjudication is the process an agency uses to decide a specific case involving specific parties. Where rulemaking looks forward and applies broadly, adjudication looks backward and applies narrowly. It resolves a particular dispute: did this company violate the law, does this person qualify for these benefits, should this license be revoked. The APA sets out procedures for adjudication just as it does for rulemaking, and just as with rulemaking, it splits the process into formal and informal versions.

Formal adjudication is the trial-type process, and it's governed by Sections 554, 556, and 557 of the APA. When it applies, the agency has to provide many of the features you'd recognize from a courtroom: notice of the charges, a hearing before an impartial presiding officer, the chance to present evidence and testimony, the right to cross-examine opposing witnesses, and a decision based on the record built at the hearing. The party facing the agency can usually be represented by a lawyer. The proceeding produces a written decision with findings of fact and conclusions of law, which can then be appealed within the agency and, eventually, to a real court.

The trigger for formal adjudication mirrors the trigger for formal rulemaking. It applies when the agency's enabling statute requires a determination to be made, in the APA's language, "on the record after opportunity for an agency hearing." Those words, or something close to them, signal that Congress wanted the full formal process. When a statute is silent or vague about the hearing, the agency generally gets to use informal procedures instead, and courts have often deferred to the agency's own reading of whether formal adjudication is required.

Informal adjudication covers everything else, and it's actually the bulk of what agencies do. The APA says surprisingly little about it. Most agency decisions, the routine determinations made every day about benefits, applications, and minor enforcement matters, happen through informal processes that the statute barely addresses. There's no required trial-type hearing, no mandated cross-examination. The procedures come from the individual agency's own rules and from whatever the Constitution's due process guarantee requires. Because informal adjudication is so common and so lightly regulated by the APA, the constitutional due process floor becomes the most important protection, and that floor is where a great deal of the law has developed.

The due process foundation. Before the APA's categories even come into play, the Constitution imposes its own requirement. The Fifth and Fourteenth Amendments say the government can't deprive a person of "life, liberty, or property" without "due process of law." When an agency's action takes away something that counts as liberty or property, the person is entitled to some kind of fair procedure, regardless of what the agency's statute says. The hard questions are two: when does due process apply, and how much process is due?

The first question, when due process applies, turns on whether the government is taking away a protected interest. Property interests include obvious things like money and physical property, but they also include benefits and entitlements a person has a legitimate claim to under the law. A professional license, once granted, can be a property interest. Government benefits a person qualifies for can be too. Liberty interests cover freedom from confinement and certain fundamental freedoms. If the agency's action reaches one of these protected interests, due process kicks in.

The landmark case on this is **Goldberg v. Kelly** in 1970. New York had been terminating welfare benefits without giving recipients a hearing beforehand. The Supreme Court held that welfare benefits are a form of property protected by due process, and that the government couldn't cut them off without first giving the recipient an evidentiary hearing. For someone dependent on welfare to survive, losing benefits by mistake could be devastating, and the Court found that the stakes demanded a hearing before the termination took effect, not after. Goldberg established that government benefits aren't a mere privilege the state can withdraw at will; they can be an entitlement that due process protects.

How much process is due. The second question, how much process, got its enduring answer in **Mathews v. Eldridge** in 1976. This case involved the termination of Social Security disability benefits, and the Court had to decide whether the recipient was entitled to a full hearing before termination, as in Goldberg, or whether a later hearing would do. The Court held that a pre-termination hearing wasn't required here, and in reaching that result it laid out a three-part balancing test that courts still use to decide how much process any given situation demands.

The Mathews test weighs three factors against each other.

Factor	Question It Asks
Private interest	How important is the interest the person stands to lose?
Risk of error	How likely is a mistaken decision under the current procedures, and would more procedure reduce that risk?
Government interest	What burden, including cost and administrative disruption, would additional procedures impose on the government?

Courts plug the specifics of a situation into these three factors and reach a conclusion about what process is constitutionally required. In Mathews itself, the Court reasoned that disability benefits, unlike welfare, don't depend on financial need, so the consequences of a temporary erroneous termination were less severe than in Goldberg. It also found that disability decisions rest largely on medical reports, which are more reliable and less dependent on live testimony than the fact questions in a welfare case, lowering the risk of error from a paper process. And it weighed the administrative cost of giving everyone a hearing before termination. Balancing these, the Court concluded a post-termination hearing was enough. The takeaway is that due process is flexible, not fixed. It demands more procedure when the stakes are high and the risk of error is real, and less when they're not.

The line between adjudication and rulemaking. One more foundational distinction shapes when a hearing is required at all, and it goes back much further than the APA. Two early cases drew a line that still matters. In **Londoner v. Denver** in 1908, the city assessed a special tax on a small group of specific property owners for paving their street. The Supreme Court held that because the assessment applied to particular individuals based on their particular circumstances, those individuals were entitled to a hearing before the tax was imposed. A few years later, in **Bi-Metallic Investment Co. v. State Board of Equalization** in 1915, Colorado raised property valuations across an entire city, affecting everyone who owned property there. The Court, in an opinion by Justice Holmes, held that no individualized hearings were required. When a government action applies generally to a large group, the Court reasoned, people's remedy is political, through the ballot and their representatives, not through individual hearings.

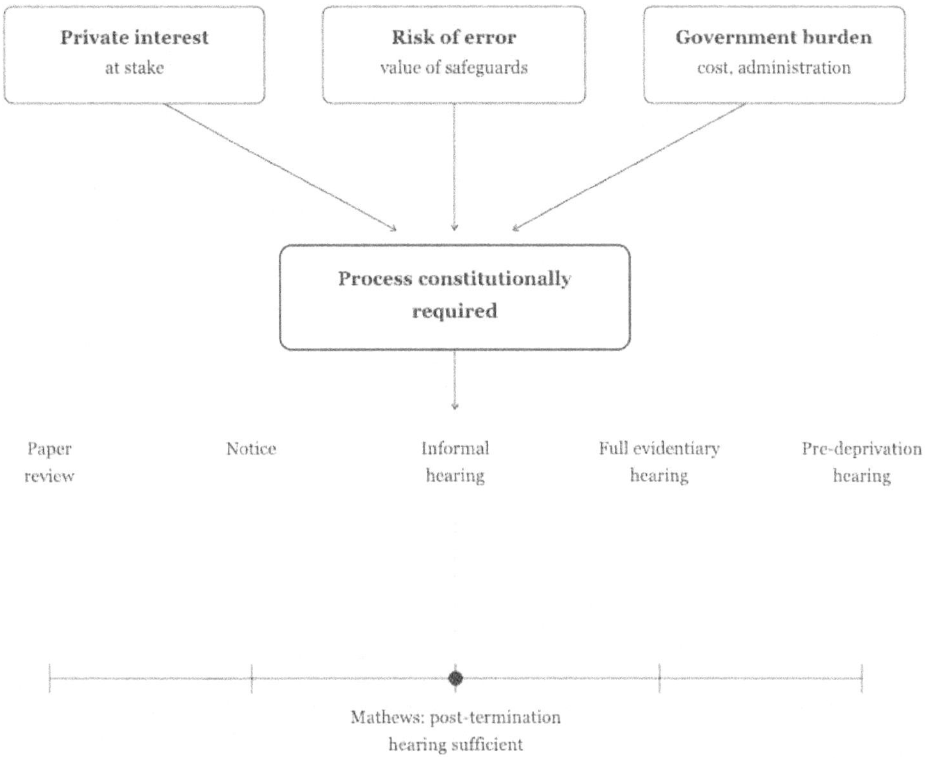

The distinction these cases drew is the same one running through this whole book: individualized decisions about specific parties (adjudication) generally require a hearing, while general decisions affecting large groups (rulemaking) don't. It would be impossible to give every affected person a personal hearing before enacting a rule that touches millions, and it would be unfair to decide one person's specific case without letting them be heard. The number of people affected and whether the action turns on facts specific to individuals are what separate the two, and they determine whether the Constitution demands a hearing.

Fairness inside the agency. Because the agency in a formal adjudication is often both the prosecutor and the judge, the APA builds in protections to keep the process fair. One is the **separation of functions**. The APA generally prohibits the people who investigated or prosecuted a case from also advising the decision-maker on that same case. The idea is to keep the adversarial side of the agency walled off from the judging side, so the official deciding the case isn't secretly the same person who built the case against you. Another protection is a ban on **ex parte communications**, meaning private, off-the-record contacts between the decision-maker and one side about the merits of the case. In a formal proceeding, the parties can't whisper in the judge's ear outside the hearing. These safeguards try to give agency adjudication some of the impartiality of a real court, even though the whole thing happens inside the agency that brought the charges. Whether they succeed, and whether internal safeguards can ever fully substitute for an independent court, is exactly the question the Supreme Court has started asking again.

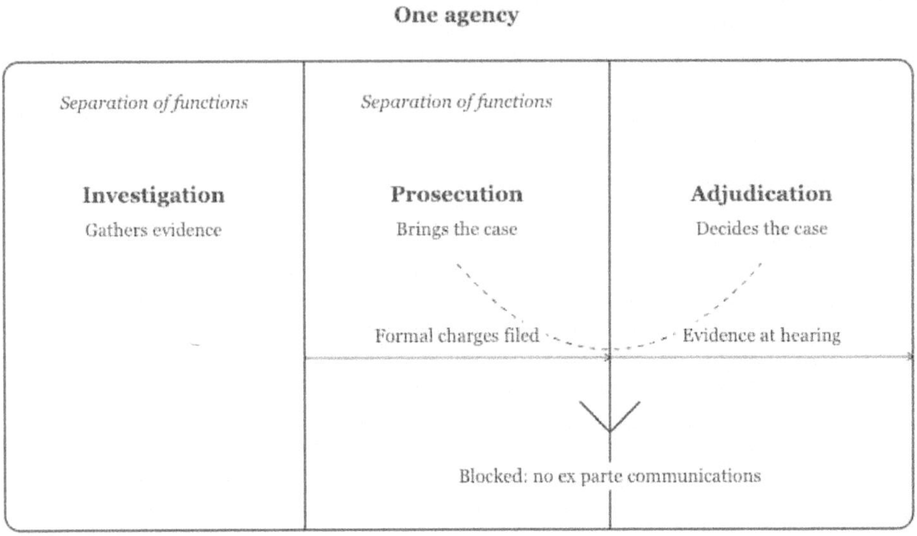

Impartiality maintained inside the agency that brought the case

Administrative Law Judges and Their Role

At the center of formal adjudication sits the **administrative law judge**, usually called an ALJ. These are the officials who preside over agency hearings, and they occupy an unusual position: they work for the agency, yet they're supposed to decide cases impartially, sometimes ruling against the very agency that employs them. There are close to 2,000 ALJs across the federal government, and they handle an enormous volume of cases, far more than the federal courts. The Social Security Administration alone employs the majority of them, deciding hundreds of thousands of disability claims a year. Others work at the SEC, the NLRB, the Federal Energy Regulatory Commission, and dozens of other agencies.

What ALJs do. An ALJ runs the hearing much as a trial judge runs a trial. The ALJ manages the proceeding, rules on evidence and objections, questions witnesses, and after the hearing issues an initial decision with findings of fact and conclusions of law. In most agencies, that initial decision isn't the final word. The agency head or a commission can review the ALJ's decision and change it, because the ultimate authority to decide the case rests with the agency, not the judge. This is a fundamental difference from the regular court system, where a trial judge's decision stands unless a higher court reverses it. An ALJ's decision is more like a recommendation that the agency's leadership can accept, modify, or reject, though it carries real weight and agencies often adopt it.

Decisional independence. Even though ALJs work for the agencies whose cases they hear, the APA gives them meaningful protections designed to keep them independent. They can't be assigned duties inconsistent with their judging role. Their pay is set by an outside body, not by the agency, so the agency can't reward or punish them financially based on how they rule. And they can't be removed at the agency's whim. Under the APA, an ALJ can be removed only for good cause, and that good cause has to be established in a proceeding before a separate body, the Merit Systems

Protection Board. This means an agency that dislikes how one of its ALJs is ruling can't simply fire the judge; it has to prove good cause to an independent tribunal. These protections give ALJs what's called decisional independence, a degree of insulation meant to let them decide cases honestly even when the honest decision goes against their employer.

That independence, though, has collided with a constitutional principle we saw earlier in this book: the president's control over the executive branch. And this is where ALJs have become the subject of major litigation.

The Lucia problem. The first collision came over how ALJs are appointed. In **Lucia v. SEC** in 2018, the Supreme Court held that the SEC's administrative law judges are "officers of the United States," not mere employees. That distinction, drawn in an earlier chapter, matters because officers have to be appointed in the specific ways the Constitution's Appointments Clause requires, while employees can just be hired through the normal civil service process. The SEC had been selecting its ALJs through ordinary hiring, and the Court held that was unconstitutional. Because ALJs exercise real authority, presiding over hearings, ruling on evidence, and issuing decisions, they had to be appointed by the head of the agency, the President, or a court, consistent with the Appointments Clause. The decision forced the SEC and other agencies to have their agency heads formally appoint their ALJs, correcting the flaw.

The removal problem. Lucia solved one constitutional issue and created another. If ALJs are officers who exercise executive power, then the same logic that limits removal protections for other officers, the logic from the removal cases in Chapter 2, might apply to them too. And here's the tension: the APA protects ALJs from removal except for good cause found by the Merit Systems Protection Board, whose own members are protected from removal. That's a layering of protections that resembles the "double for-cause" structure the Court struck down in Free Enterprise Fund. If an ALJ is protected from removal except for cause, and the body that decides that cause is itself protected, then the president is several steps removed from any control over the ALJ. Whether this layered protection for ALJs is constitutional remains an open and contested question, one the courts are actively working through. The very independence that makes ALJs impartial is the feature that puts them in constitutional jeopardy.

The Jarkesy earthquake. The biggest challenge to the whole system arrived in **SEC v. Jarkesy** in 2024, and its reasoning reaches beyond ALJs to the fundamental question of whether agencies can adjudicate certain cases at all. The SEC had charged George Jarkesy with securities fraud and pursued the case in its own in-house forum before one of its ALJs, seeking civil penalties. Jarkesy argued that the Constitution entitled him to a jury trial in a real federal court, and that the SEC couldn't force him into agency adjudication. The Supreme Court agreed, in a decision written by Chief Justice Roberts.

The Court's reasoning rested on the Seventh Amendment, which preserves the right to a jury trial in "suits at common law." When the government sues someone for civil penalties based on fraud, the Court held, that's essentially a legal action of the kind that historically required a jury. Securities fraud closely resembles common-law fraud, and the penalties the SEC sought were the kind of remedy courts of law traditionally provided. So the defendant had a right to have the case heard by a jury in an Article III court, not resolved by an agency's own judge.

The SEC had leaned on something called the **public rights doctrine**, an exception that allows certain matters to be adjudicated by agencies without juries. The doctrine has historically covered things like benefits determinations, immigration, and disputes over rights that exist only because the government created them. The SEC argued that its enforcement actions fell within this exception, pointing to a 1977 case, Atlas Roofing, that had allowed OSHA to impose penalties through agency adjudication without a jury. The Court in Jarkesy rejected the argument. It held that an action to enforce a fraud prohibition and impose civil penalties involves private rights of the sort that require a jury, and it read the public rights exception narrowly, distinguishing the earlier cases rather than following them. The result is that the SEC can no longer pursue civil penalties for fraud in its own courts; it has to go to federal court, where the defendant gets a jury.

Here's how the recent ALJ cases stack up.

Case	Year	Issue	Holding
Lucia v. SEC	2018	Are ALJs officers who must be properly appointed?	Yes; ALJs must be appointed under the Appointments Clause
Free Enterprise Fund	2010	Is layered removal protection valid?	No (in that context); raised doubts about ALJ removal protections
SEC v. Jarkesy	2024	Can the SEC seek civil fraud penalties in its own forum?	No; the Seventh Amendment requires a jury trial in federal court

The implications of Jarkesy are still unfolding, and they could be large. Many agencies, not just the SEC, use in-house adjudication to impose penalties, and the decision calls into question how many of those proceedings can continue when the penalties resemble the kind of relief that historically demanded a jury. Agencies may have to shift more of their enforcement into federal court, which is slower, more expensive, and more resource-intensive than the in-house process they've relied on. The whole model of agencies acting as their own courts, efficient but constitutionally awkward, is being reexamined, and ALJs sit right at the center of the reexamination.

Consent Decrees and Settlement Agreements

For all the attention that hearings and trials get, the reality of enforcement is that most cases never reach a decision at all. They settle. Just as the vast majority of civil lawsuits end in settlement rather than trial, the vast majority of agency enforcement actions end in a negotiated agreement between the agency and the party it's pursuing. Understanding settlement is understanding how enforcement actually works day to day, because the hearing is the exception and the deal is the rule.

Settlements in the enforcement context take a couple of forms.

A **consent decree** is a settlement that gets entered as a court order, which means a judge approves it and it carries the enforceability of a judicial judgment. If the party violates the decree later, it can be held in contempt of court.

A **consent order** is similar but stays within the agency, approved by the agency rather than a court. Both accomplish the same basic thing: the party agrees to do certain things, stop doing others, and often pay a penalty, in exchange for resolving the matter without a full-blown adjudication.

A common feature of these settlements is the **"neither admit nor deny" provision**. Under this arrangement, the settling party agrees to the terms and pays whatever penalty is imposed, but doesn't formally admit that it did anything wrong. This lets the party resolve the case without creating an admission of liability that could be used against it in related private lawsuits. Agencies have historically accepted these provisions because they allow cases to settle quickly, though they've drawn criticism from people who argue that letting wrongdoers pay a penalty without admitting fault lets them off too easily and hides the truth from the public. The SEC in particular has faced pressure over its use of "neither admit nor deny" settlements, and at times it has required admissions in especially serious cases.

Why do parties settle, and why do agencies? Both sides usually come out ahead. For the party facing enforcement, settling brings certainty and control. A hearing is expensive, its outcome is uncertain, and losing could mean a larger penalty plus the reputational damage of a formal finding of wrongdoing. Settling caps the downside and ends the matter. For the agency, settlement conserves resources. Agencies have limited budgets and staff, and they can't possibly litigate every case to conclusion. Settling frees them to pursue more violations with the resources they have, and it produces a reliable result rather than gambling on a hearing. The efficiency is why settlement dominates: both sides generally prefer a known, negotiated outcome to the cost and risk of fighting it out.

There's a tradeoff hidden in all this settling, and it's worth naming. When most enforcement ends in negotiated deals rather than adjudicated decisions, the law develops less through public rulings and more through private bargains. Each settlement resolves one case but sets no precedent and creates no public record of what the law requires. Critics worry this makes enforcement less transparent and less accountable, because the standards agencies actually apply get worked out in negotiations rather than announced in decisions anyone can read and challenge. The efficiency of settlement, in other words, comes at some cost to the public's ability to see and scrutinize how agencies wield their power.

Civil Penalties and Fines

When agencies enforce the law, the most common weapon they reach for is money. **Civil penalties**, also called civil fines, are monetary sanctions imposed for violations, and they're the workhorse of administrative enforcement. As noted earlier in this book, these penalties are civil, not criminal, which means they don't carry jail time and don't come with the full array of criminal procedural protections. They do carry real financial consequences, sometimes enormous ones, and for many businesses the threat of civil penalties is the main thing that keeps them following the rules.

How penalties get set. Enabling statutes typically authorize civil penalties and set the terms, and the structures vary. Some statutes set a fixed penalty for a violation. Others set a maximum and let the agency decide the amount within that ceiling based on the circumstances. A common and powerful structure is the **per-violation, per-day penalty**, where the statute authorizes a penalty for each violation and for each day the violation continues. This structure can generate staggering totals. A company that violates an environmental standard might face a penalty of tens of thousands of dollars per day, and if the violation went on for months across multiple sites, the arithmetic produces figures in the millions. The per-day feature is deliberate: it pressures companies to fix violations fast, because every day of delay adds to the bill.

Agencies usually consider a set of factors in deciding how large a penalty should be within the statutory range. These commonly include the seriousness of the violation, whether the party acted in good faith or deliberately, the party's history of prior violations, the economic benefit the party gained by breaking the rule, and the party's ability to pay. The economic benefit factor matters because a penalty smaller than the money a company saved by violating the law would just be a cost of doing business; agencies try to set penalties high enough to remove any profit from noncompliance.

Disgorgement. Beyond penalties, agencies sometimes seek **disgorgement**, which is an order requiring a wrongdoer to give up the profits it gained from illegal conduct. Disgorgement isn't technically a penalty; it's meant to take away ill-gotten gains rather than to punish. The SEC has used disgorgement heavily in securities cases, forcing violators to surrender the money they made through fraud or other violations.

The Supreme Court has clarified the limits of this tool in recent years. In **Kokesh v. SEC** in 2017, the Court held that disgorgement functions as a penalty for purposes of the statute of limitations, meaning the SEC can't reach back indefinitely to recover old gains. In **Liu v. SEC** in 2020, the Court held that disgorgement is permissible as a form of equitable relief but limited it, requiring that the amount generally be tied to the wrongdoer's net profits and that the money typically go to the victims rather than to the government. These decisions reined in a tool the SEC had used expansively.

On the next page is a summary of the main monetary tools.

Tool	Purpose	Nature
Fixed penalty	Sanction a violation at a set amount	Punitive
Discretionary penalty	Sanction within a statutory range based on circumstances	Punitive
Per-day penalty	Pressure fast correction; accrues daily	Punitive
Disgorgement	Strip profits gained from illegal conduct	Remedial, though treated as a penalty in some contexts

The jury trial question, again. Civil penalties connect back to the Seventh Amendment issue that drove Jarkesy, and the connection runs deeper than one case. Well before Jarkesy, the Court had held in **Tull v. United States** in 1987 that when the government sues for civil penalties in federal court, the defendant is entitled to a jury trial to determine liability, because an action for civil penalties is the kind of legal action the Seventh Amendment covers. Tull involved the Clean Water Act, and it established that civil penalties, despite being called civil, trigger the jury right when the government pursues them in court. Jarkesy extended the logic to the question of forum, holding that the government can't escape the jury requirement by pursuing the penalties in an agency's own tribunal instead of a court. Together, these cases mean that the government's power to impose civil penalties for conduct resembling common-law wrongs comes tied to a constitutional right to a jury, a right agencies can't sidestep by keeping the case in-house. This is a live constraint on enforcement, and it's pushing agencies to rethink how and where they seek monetary sanctions.

Licensing and Permitting Decisions

A huge amount of what agencies do involves saying yes or no to permission. Before you can broadcast on a radio frequency, discharge wastewater into a river, practice medicine, sell securities, or operate a nuclear plant, some agency has to grant you a license or a permit. And once granted, that permission can be renewed, modified, suspended, or revoked. These licensing and permitting decisions are a form of adjudication, because each one is an individualized determination about a specific applicant, and they carry their own body of legal rules.

Licenses as gatekeeping. Licensing gives agencies control over entry into regulated activities. The Federal Communications Commission grants licenses to use the broadcast spectrum, deciding who gets to operate a television or radio station on a given frequency. Because the spectrum is limited and can't accommodate everyone, the FCC's licensing power is a form of rationing a scarce public resource. The Nuclear Regulatory Commission licenses nuclear power plants, a process so demanding that obtaining a license can take years and enormous expense, reflecting the stakes involved. Professional licensing, though usually handled at the state level, works the same way: a board decides who meets the qualifications to practice a profession, and without the license, a person can't legally do the work.

The power to grant a license is also the power to attach conditions to it. Agencies frequently issue licenses subject to requirements the holder must follow, and violating those conditions can lead to the license being suspended or revoked. This gives the agency ongoing control over the licensed activity, not just a one-time yes-or-no decision. A broadcaster operates under conditions the FCC sets; a facility operates under conditions in its permit. The license becomes a tool for continuous regulation, with the threat of revocation backing it up.

Permits and the environment. Environmental regulation runs heavily on permits. Under the Clean Water Act, a facility that discharges pollutants into the nation's waters must obtain a permit through the National Pollutant Discharge Elimination System, which sets limits on what the facility can release and requires monitoring and reporting. Under the Clean Air Act, major sources of air pollution need permits governing their emissions. These permitting systems are how broad environmental statutes get applied to individual facilities. The statute and the agency's rules set the general standards; the permit translates them into specific obligations for a specific plant, tailored to its situation. Getting a permit, or fighting the conditions in one, is often where the real regulatory action happens for a regulated business, more so than the underlying rule.

Due process in taking a license away. Granting a license and revoking one aren't treated the same under the law, and the difference comes from the due process principles discussed earlier. An applicant seeking a license for the first time generally has weaker procedural rights, because the applicant doesn't yet have anything the government is taking away. But once an agency has granted a license, the holder often has a property interest in it, which means the agency can't revoke it without due process. Revoking a professional's license can destroy their livelihood, and courts have recognized that such a deprivation typically requires notice and a hearing before it takes effect. So the procedural protections are strongest when the agency moves to take away a license someone already holds, and weaker when someone is merely applying. This tracks the logic of Goldberg and Mathews: the more a person stands to lose of something they already have, the more process they're owed before losing it.

The distinction between granting and revoking matters in practice, so here it is directly.

Action	Interest at Stake	Typical Process
Denying a new application	Applicant has no existing entitlement	Weaker; often no full hearing required
Renewing a license	Holder may have reliance interest	Moderate; depends on the scheme

Revoking or suspending	Holder has a property interest	Strong; usually notice and a hearing before deprivation

Investigative Powers and Subpoena Authority

Before an agency can bring an enforcement action, decide a case, or impose a penalty, it needs to know what happened. That's what investigative power is for. Agencies have broad authority to gather information: to demand documents, compel testimony, require reports, and inspect premises. These investigative tools are the foundation of enforcement, because without the power to find out what regulated parties are doing, an agency couldn't tell whether the law is being followed. And because these powers involve the government demanding things from private parties, they run into constitutional limits, particularly the Fourth Amendment's protection against unreasonable searches.

Administrative subpoenas. The core investigative tool is the **administrative subpoena**, an agency demand that a party produce documents or provide testimony. Agencies can issue these subpoenas as part of an investigation, and their reach is wide. The foundational case is **Oklahoma Press Publishing Co. v. Walling** in 1946, where the Supreme Court upheld an agency's subpoena power and set the standard for when such subpoenas are enforceable. The Court held that an administrative subpoena is valid if the investigation is for a legitimate purpose, the information sought is relevant to that purpose, and the demand is reasonable and not too indefinite or burdensome. This is a fairly forgiving standard, and it gives agencies substantial power to compel information.

Just how forgiving the standard is became clear in **United States v. Morton Salt Co.** in 1950. The Court held that an agency doesn't need probable cause or even a specific suspicion of wrongdoing to investigate. It can investigate simply to satisfy itself that regulated parties are complying with the law, acting on what the Court memorably described as a kind of official curiosity. An agency, the Court said, can investigate merely on the suspicion that the law is being violated, or even just to be sure that it isn't. This means agencies can demand information without the kind of justification a criminal investigator would need, reflecting the idea that regulated businesses accept a degree of oversight as the price of operating in a regulated field. The standard for enforcing an administrative subpoena is therefore much lower than the standard for a search warrant in a criminal case.

Physical inspections and the Fourth Amendment. Investigative power gets more constitutionally sensitive when it involves physically entering and searching a business's premises. Here the Fourth Amendment's warrant requirement comes into play, though in a modified form. The leading case is **Marshall v. Barlow's, Inc.** in 1978, where an OSHA inspector tried to enter a business to conduct a safety inspection without a warrant, and the owner refused. The Supreme Court held that OSHA generally needs a warrant to inspect a business over the owner's objection, rejecting the government's claim that it could inspect workplaces at will. But the Court also held that the warrant standard for an administrative inspection is lower than for a criminal search. The agency doesn't need probable cause to believe a violation exists; it can get an inspection warrant by showing that the business was selected according to reasonable, neutral criteria, such as a general administrative plan for inspecting workplaces. So administrative inspections do require warrants as a rule, but the warrants are easier to obtain than criminal ones.

There's an exception to even this modified warrant requirement, and it covers **closely regulated industries**. For businesses in industries with a long history of pervasive regulation, where operators have a reduced expectation of privacy, agencies can sometimes conduct warrantless inspections. The Court applied this in **New York v. Burger** in 1987, upholding a warrantless inspection of a vehicle dismantling business. The reasoning is that some industries are so heavily regulated that anyone operating in them knows they're subject to inspection, so a warrantless search doesn't violate a reasonable expectation of privacy the way it would for an ordinary business or a home. This exception is limited to genuinely closely regulated fields, and the Court has been reluctant to expand the category, but where it applies, it lets agencies inspect without the warrant that Barlow's would otherwise require.

Tool	What It Does	Standard / Limit
Administrative subpoena	Compels documents or testimony	Legitimate purpose, relevant, reasonable (Oklahoma Press); no suspicion needed (Morton Salt)
Reporting requirement	Requires parties to submit information regularly	Must be authorized by statute and reasonable
Routine inspection	Physical examination of premises	Warrant generally required, but on a lower standard (Barlow's)
Closely regulated industry inspection	Inspection of pervasively regulated business	Warrantless inspection permitted (Burger)

Reporting and recordkeeping. Beyond subpoenas and inspections, agencies gather information through **reporting and recordkeeping requirements**. Many regulatory schemes require regulated parties to keep certain records and submit regular reports to the agency. Public companies file disclosures with the SEC. Employers keep records OSHA can examine. Facilities monitor their emissions and report the results to environmental agencies. These requirements shift much of the information-gathering burden onto the regulated parties themselves, requiring them to document their own compliance and hand the documentation to the agency. This is often more efficient than having the agency go out and investigate, and it creates a paper trail the agency can review and, if necessary, use as the basis for enforcement. The obligation to self-report is backed by the threat of penalties for false or missing reports, which gives parties a strong reason to keep accurate records and tell the truth.

Taken together, these investigative powers give agencies substantial reach into the affairs of regulated parties. An agency can demand documents on little more than a desire to check compliance, require detailed ongoing reports, and inspect premises under a relaxed warrant standard or, in some industries, no warrant at all. These powers are what make enforcement possible, and they reflect a basic bargain of the regulatory state: those who operate in regulated fields accept a level of governmental scrutiny that ordinary citizens don't face, in exchange for the privilege of doing business in areas the public has decided need oversight. The constitutional limits that exist, mainly from the Fourth Amendment, temper these powers at the edges but leave agencies with wide latitude to find out what they need to know.

Discussion Question

For decades, agencies like the SEC resolved most enforcement cases in their own courtrooms, before their own judges, without juries, and the system worked efficiently because of it. In Jarkesy, the Supreme Court decided that efficiency doesn't justify denying people the jury trial the Constitution promises when the government comes after them for something that looks like fraud.

If forcing these cases into real courts makes enforcement so slow and costly that agencies simply pursue fewer violations, has the country traded one kind of unfairness for another? Where would you strike the balance between giving accused parties the full protection of an independent court and giving agencies the practical ability to enforce the law at all?

Chapter 6: Judicial Review of Agency Action

A group of Atlantic herring fishermen off the coast of New England got tired of paying for a stranger to ride along on their boats. Federal fisheries rules required them to carry government-approved monitors who observed their catch, and worse, required the fishermen to cover the cost of those monitors themselves, running to roughly 700 dollars a day. The statute said the agency could require observers. It said nothing about who had to pay for them. The agency read its own silence as permission to make the fishermen foot the bill.

So the fishermen sued. Their case was, on its face, a small dispute about a few hundred dollars a day in a niche industry. It became one of the most consequential administrative law decisions in forty years. When the Supreme Court decided *Loper Bright Enterprises v. Raimondo* in 2024, it didn't just rule on herring monitors. It overturned the single most cited doctrine in the entire field, the rule that had governed how courts review agency interpretations of law since 1984. The fishermen's complaint about an unwanted passenger ended up rewriting the relationship between agencies and the courts.

That story sits at the center of this chapter, because judicial review is the check that turns agency power from something nearly absolute into something answerable. Congress creates agencies and hands them authority, but the courts decide whether agencies stayed within it. Every rule an agency writes, every case it decides, every penalty it imposes can potentially be challenged before a judge. This chapter is about how that challenge works: who's allowed to bring one, how much deference courts owe agencies on questions of law, how closely courts scrutinize agency reasoning, and when a person has to wait before going to court at all.

Standing to Sue an Agency

Before a court will look at whether an agency acted lawfully, it has to decide whether the person complaining is even entitled to be there. That threshold question is **standing**, and it trips up more challenges than any other single doctrine. Standing asks whether the plaintiff has a sufficient stake in the dispute to bring it into court. The requirement comes from Article III of the Constitution, which limits federal courts to deciding actual "cases" and "controversies," not abstract grievances about how the government is run. You can't sue an agency just because you think it's doing something wrong. You have to show that its action affects you in a particular way.

The three requirements. The definitive statement of what standing requires comes from *Lujan v. Defenders of Wildlife* in 1992, an opinion by Justice Scalia that laid out a three-part test every plaintiff has to satisfy. The three elements are injury in fact, causation, and redressability, and a plaintiff who misses any one of them has no standing and gets thrown out before the merits are ever reached.

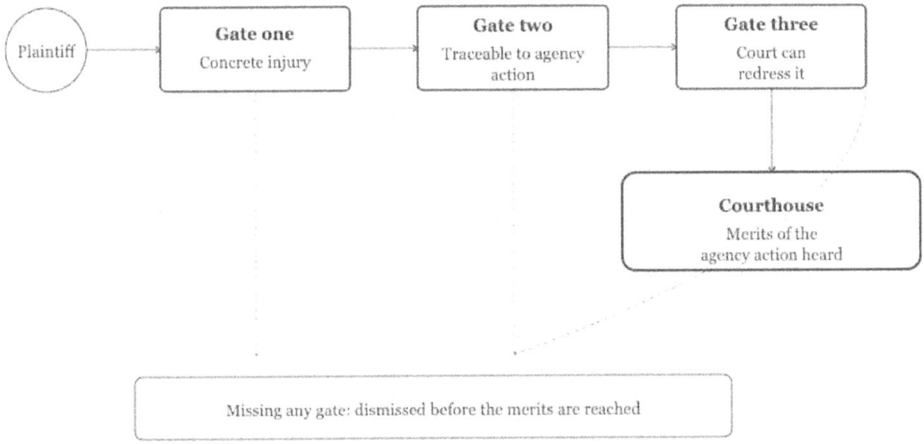

Element	What the Plaintiff Must Show
Injury in fact	A concrete and particularized harm that is actual or imminent, not conjectural or hypothetical
Causation	The injury is fairly traceable to the challenged agency action, not the result of some third party not before the court
Redressability	A favorable court decision would likely remedy the injury

Each element does real work. **Injury in fact** means the plaintiff has to have suffered or be about to suffer an actual harm. A general interest in seeing the law enforced isn't enough; the harm has to be particular to the plaintiff. In *Lujan* itself, environmental groups challenged a rule interpreting the Endangered Species Act, claiming injury because their members intended to travel abroad someday to observe endangered species affected by the rule. The Court found that "someday" intentions, with no concrete plans, didn't amount to imminent injury. The plaintiffs cared about the issue, but caring isn't being harmed.

Causation requires that the agency's action actually caused the injury, rather than some independent actor. If the harm flows from the decisions of third parties who aren't in the case, and the connection to the agency is too attenuated, causation fails. **Redressability** requires that winning the case would actually fix the problem. If a court ruling in the plaintiff's favor wouldn't relieve the injury, because the harm would persist regardless, there's no point in the court deciding, and standing is absent.

How strictly the injury requirement bites. The Court has kept the injury requirement demanding, and a line of cases shows how. In *Clapper v. Amnesty International* in 2013, plaintiffs challenged a surveillance law, claiming their communications might be intercepted. The Court held that a speculative fear of future surveillance wasn't the kind of certainly impending injury standing requires; the plaintiffs couldn't show their communications actually would be intercepted, only that they might be. In *Spokeo, Inc. v. Robins* in 2016 and again in *TransUnion LLC v. Ramirez* in 2021, the Court addressed whether a bare violation of a statutory right, without concrete harm, gives standing. It held that a plaintiff must show a concrete injury even when a statute has been violated. Congress can create legal rights, but it can't manufacture standing by letting people sue over violations that caused them no real harm. *TransUnion* put it directly: no concrete harm, no standing.

Special rules for states. States sometimes get treated more generously on standing than private plaintiffs, and this connects to a case discussed earlier in this book for a different reason. In *Massachusetts v. EPA* in 2007, several states challenged the EPA's refusal to regulate greenhouse gases. On the standing question, the Court held that Massachusetts had standing to sue, and it gave the state what it called "special solicitude" in the standing analysis. The state's injury was the loss of coastal land to rising seas caused by climate change, and although that injury was diffuse and shared with many others, the Court found it sufficient for a state asserting its interests as a sovereign and a landowner. This special treatment for states remains somewhat contested, but it reflects the idea that states occupy a different position than individual plaintiffs when they come to court to challenge federal action.

Associational and organizational standing. Groups often want to sue on behalf of their members, and a separate doctrine governs when they can. Under the test from *Hunt v. Washington State Apple Advertising Commission* in 1977, an organization has standing to sue on behalf of its members when its members would have standing to sue in their own right, the interests at stake are relevant to the organization's purpose, and neither the claim nor the relief requires the individual members to participate in the lawsuit. This lets advocacy organizations, trade associations, and unions bring challenges without every affected member having to join. An environmental group can sue over a rule that harms its members' use of a natural area, as long as at least one identifiable member would have standing personally.

The zone of interests. Beyond the constitutional requirements, there's an additional test that comes from the APA rather than the Constitution, sometimes called prudential standing.

A plaintiff challenging agency action generally has to fall within the **zone of interests** the relevant statute protects. This means the plaintiff's interest has to be the kind of interest Congress had in mind when it passed the law, not some interest wholly unrelated to the statute's purpose. The idea, from *Association of Data Processing Service Organizations v. Camp* in 1970, is that a person can invoke a statute only if they're the kind of person the statute was meant to protect or regulate. The zone-of-interests test is generally applied leniently, and the Court has clarified that it isn't a constitutional requirement but a question of whether Congress intended to allow this type of plaintiff to sue under this particular law.

Standing, taken together, is the gate every challenger has to pass through, and it's a real barrier. Many people with genuine objections to what agencies do never get their objections heard, because they can't show the particular, concrete, redressable injury the doctrine demands. The requirement channels judicial review toward those actually affected and keeps courts out of abstract policy disputes, but it also means that some agency actions escape review simply because no one can show the kind of harm that opens the courthouse door.

The Chevron Doctrine and Its Legacy

For forty years, the most important question in administrative law was how much courts should defer to an agency's reading of the statutes it administers, and for all of those forty years, the answer had a name: **Chevron deference**. The doctrine shaped tens of thousands of cases, defined the balance of power between agencies and courts, and became the single most cited decision in the field. Then, in 2024, the Supreme Court overruled it. Understanding what Chevron was, how it worked, and why it fell is understanding the central drama of modern administrative law.

Where Chevron came from. The doctrine takes its name from *Chevron U.S.A., Inc. v. Natural Resources Defense Council* in 1984, a case that, ironically, no one at the time recognized as a landmark. It involved the EPA's interpretation of the term "stationary source" under the Clean Air Act, a technical question about how to count sources of pollution at an industrial facility. The EPA had adopted a particular reading, environmental groups challenged it, and the Supreme Court had to decide whether to accept the agency's interpretation. In doing so, the Court announced a framework that would govern statutory interpretation questions for a generation.

The two-step framework. Chevron set up a two-step analysis for reviewing an agency's interpretation of a statute it administers, and the two steps became so familiar that lawyers referred to them by number.

At **Step One**, the court asks whether Congress has directly spoken to the precise question at issue. If the statute is clear, that's the end of it. Both the court and the agency have to follow the unambiguous meaning of the statute. The agency gets no deference on a question Congress already answered, because there's nothing to interpret.

At **Step Two**, if the statute is silent or ambiguous on the question, the court doesn't impose its own reading. Instead, it asks only whether the agency's interpretation is a reasonable or permissible construction of the statute. If the agency's reading is reasonable, the court defers to it, even if the court would have chosen a different interpretation on its own. This was the heart of Chevron: when a statute is ambiguous, the agency, not the court, gets to decide what it means, so long as the agency's choice is reasonable.

Step	Question	Result
Step One	Has Congress directly addressed the precise question?	If yes, the clear statutory meaning controls; no deference

Step Two	If the statute is ambiguous, is the agency's interpretation reasonable?	If yes, the court defers to the agency's reading

The theory behind deference. Why should courts defer to agencies on questions of statutory meaning? Chevron offered two justifications. One was about congressional intent: when Congress leaves a gap or an ambiguity in a statute it assigns an agency to administer, that ambiguity can be understood as an implicit delegation to the agency to fill the gap. Congress, the theory went, would rather have the expert agency resolve the ambiguity than have generalist judges do it. The other justification was about political accountability. Agencies answer, through the president, to the electorate, while judges don't. When a statute leaves a genuine policy choice open, the argument ran, it's better for that choice to be made by an accountable agency than by unelected courts. Filling statutory gaps often involves policy judgment, and Chevron said policy judgment belongs to the politically accountable branch.

For decades, this framework held, and it had enormous consequences. Chevron made agencies powerful, because it meant that whenever a statute was less than perfectly clear, and statutes are often unclear, the agency's interpretation would usually prevail. Regulated parties challenging agency rules faced an uphill fight: they couldn't just argue the agency's reading was wrong; they had to show it was unreasonable, a much harder standard. Chevron became a thumb on the scale in favor of agencies in countless disputes.

Step Zero and the limits. Over time, the Court added qualifications that narrowed when Chevron even applied, and these became known collectively as "Step Zero," the threshold question of whether Chevron governs at all. The most important came in *United States v. Mead Corp.* in 2001, which held that Chevron deference applies only when Congress delegated authority to the agency to make rules carrying the force of law, and the agency issued its interpretation in the exercise of that authority. Formal rules and formal adjudications generally qualified. Informal agency documents, like opinion letters and guidance, often didn't. When Chevron didn't apply, courts fell back on a weaker form of deference from an older case, *Skidmore v. Swift & Co.* in 1944.

Skidmore respect. Skidmore deference is worth understanding on its own, because it survived when Chevron didn't. Under *Skidmore*, a court gives an agency's interpretation weight based on its persuasiveness, considering factors like the thoroughness of the agency's reasoning, the consistency of its position over time, and the agency's expertise. Skidmore isn't really deference in the binding sense; it's respect. The court makes its own decision but takes the agency's views seriously to the extent they're well-reasoned and consistent. A persuasive agency interpretation carries the day under Skidmore because it's persuasive, not because the court is required to accept it. This weaker standard is the one that now governs, as we'll see.

Deference to an agency's own rules. A related but distinct form of deference deserves mention. **Auer deference**, from *Auer v. Robbins* in 1997 (building on *Bowles v. Seminole Rock* in 1945), requires courts to defer to an agency's interpretation of its own ambiguous regulations. This is different from Chevron, which concerns interpreting statutes; Auer concerns interpreting the agency's own regulatory text. Critics attacked Auer for giving agencies an incentive to write vague rules and then interpret them however they liked, effectively letting the agency both write and construe the law. The Court confronted these criticisms in *Kisor v. Wilkie* in 2019 and, rather than overruling Auer, narrowed it significantly. After *Kisor*, Auer deference applies only when the regulation is genuinely ambiguous after the court has exhausted the ordinary tools of interpretation, the agency's reading is reasonable, and several other conditions are met. Auer survived, but on a much shorter leash.

The cracks widen. By the 2010s, Chevron was under sustained attack, and the criticism came from several directions. Some justices argued that Chevron violated the APA, which says in Section 706 that courts, not agencies, "shall decide all relevant questions of law." If the APA assigns legal interpretation to courts, the argument ran, Chevron's command to defer to agencies on legal questions couldn't be squared with the statute. Others argued that Chevron let agencies aggrandize their own power by exploiting statutory ambiguity, and that it undermined the judiciary's constitutional role of saying what the law is. Still others pointed out that Chevron had become unpredictable in practice, with courts manipulating the "ambiguity" question to reach whatever result they preferred.

The Court began signaling discomfort even before it acted. In *King v. Burwell* in 2015, a case about tax credits under the Affordable Care Act, the Court faced a question of enormous economic and political importance and simply declined to apply Chevron, deciding the statutory question itself instead. It reasoned that a question this consequential wasn't the kind Congress would have implicitly delegated to an agency. That reasoning became the seed of the major questions doctrine, which holds that on issues of vast economic and political significance, courts won't assume Congress delegated the decision to an agency without a clear statement. That doctrine grew into a substantial force in its own right, and Chapter 9 takes it up in detail. Here, the point is that even before Chevron fell, the Court had started carving out the biggest and most important cases from its reach.

Loper Bright overrules Chevron. The end came in *Loper Bright Enterprises v. Raimondo* in 2024, the herring fishermen's case. Chief Justice Roberts wrote for the Court, and the holding was direct: Chevron is overruled. Courts must exercise their own independent judgment in deciding whether an agency has acted within its statutory authority, and they may not defer to an agency's interpretation of the law simply because a statute is ambiguous.

The Court's reasoning rested heavily on the APA. Section 706 directs courts to decide all relevant questions of law and to interpret statutory provisions. That command, the Court held, is incompatible with a rule requiring judges to defer to agencies on those very questions. Interpreting statutes is the judiciary's job, and Chevron had improperly handed part of that job to agencies. The Court also rejected Chevron's central premise, the idea that statutory ambiguity signals an implicit delegation to the agency. Ambiguity, the Court said, is not a delegation; it's just ambiguity, and it's the court's responsibility to resolve it using the ordinary tools of interpretation.

Importantly, the Court didn't discard agency expertise entirely. It preserved Skidmore respect, meaning courts can still consider an agency's interpretation and give it weight to the extent it's persuasive. And it held that when Congress explicitly delegates authority to an agency to define a term or fill in a specific gap, courts respect that delegation and review only whether the agency stayed within the boundaries of the delegated authority. So agencies retain a role, and genuine delegations still matter. What changed is the default: courts no longer defer to agency legal interpretations just because a statute is unclear. The agency's reading gets respect based on its quality, not automatic acceptance based on ambiguity.

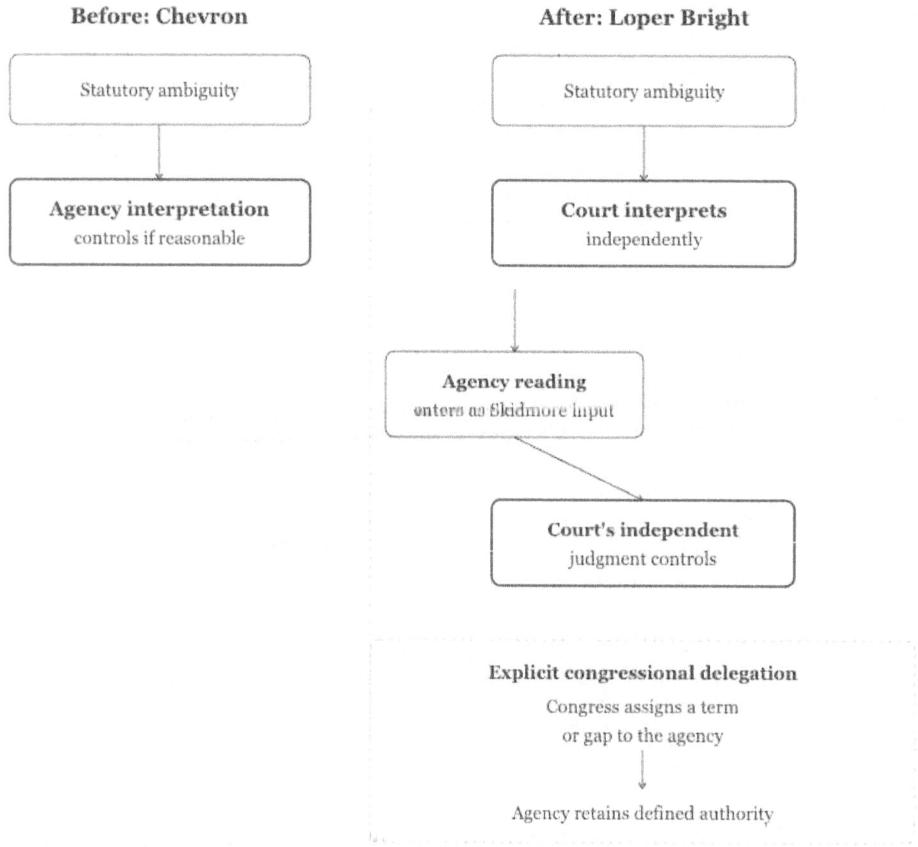

Here's the shift in a nutshell.

Aspect	Under Chevron (1984–2024)	After Loper Bright (2024)
Ambiguous statute	Court defers to any reasonable agency reading	Court decides the meaning independently

Basis for deference	Ambiguity implies delegation	Ambiguity implies nothing; court interprets
Agency expertise	Could bind the court at Step Two	Considered for persuasiveness (Skidmore)
Explicit delegation	Deference within the delegation	Still respected; court checks the boundaries
Who says what the law is	Often the agency	The court

What the overruling means. *Loper Bright* shifts interpretive power from agencies back to courts. Under Chevron, an agency facing an ambiguous statute could usually make its interpretation stick. Now, that same agency has to persuade a court that its reading is the best one, not merely a permissible one. This makes agency interpretations more vulnerable and gives regulated parties a better chance when they challenge them. It also means that the meaning of a statute is more likely to stay fixed rather than shifting when a new administration adopts a different interpretation, because the court's independent reading, once established, doesn't bend to the agency's changing views. The full consequences are still working themselves out, and Chapter 9 returns to what agency authority looks like in this new environment. For now, the takeaway is that a forty-year era ended, and the courts reclaimed the final word on what the laws agencies administer actually mean.

Arbitrary and Capricious Review

Deciding what a statute means is one kind of review. Deciding whether an agency's action was reasonable is another, and it's the workhorse of judicial review, the standard that governs the most agency decisions. It comes from Section 706 of the APA, which directs courts to set aside agency actions that are "arbitrary, capricious, an abuse of discretion, or otherwise not in accordance with law." That phrase, **arbitrary and capricious**, is the standard courts apply when reviewing the substance of an agency's discretionary choices, and while it sounds deferential, courts have given it real teeth.

What the standard demands. Arbitrary and capricious review isn't about whether the court agrees with the agency's decision. It's about whether the agency made its decision reasonably, based on the relevant evidence and considerations, and explained itself adequately. The court doesn't substitute its own policy judgment for the agency's; it checks whether the agency did its job properly. The foundational articulation comes from *Citizens to Preserve Overton Park v. Volpe* in 1971, where the Court described the inquiry as whether the agency's decision was based on a consideration of the relevant factors and whether there was a clear error of judgment. The court reviews the whole administrative record the agency compiled and asks whether the decision holds up.

The State Farm framework. The case that gave arbitrary and capricious review its modern shape is *Motor Vehicle Manufacturers Association v. State Farm Mutual Automobile Insurance Co.* in 1983. The case involved the rescission of a rule requiring passive restraints, airbags or automatic seatbelts, in new cars. A previous administration had adopted the requirement; a new administration rescinded it. The Court reviewed the rescission and struck it down as arbitrary and capricious, and in doing so it spelled out the ways an agency decision can fail the test.

Under *State Farm*, an agency acts arbitrarily and capriciously if it does any of the following:

- Relies on factors Congress didn't intend it to consider
- Entirely fails to consider an important aspect of the problem
- Offers an explanation that runs counter to the evidence before the agency
- Gives an explanation so implausible that it can't be attributed to a difference in view or agency expertise

In *State Farm* itself, the agency had rescinded the passive restraint rule without adequately considering an obvious alternative. If automatic seatbelts could be detached and airbags couldn't, the agency should at least have considered requiring airbags alone rather than scrapping the whole rule. By ignoring that alternative and failing to explain its reasoning, the agency failed the arbitrary and capricious standard. The decision established what's often called **hard look review**: the court takes a hard look to make sure the agency itself took a hard look at the problem, genuinely engaging with the evidence and the alternatives rather than acting on whim or unexplained preference.

Reasoned explanation is everything. The thread running through arbitrary and capricious review is that agencies have to explain themselves. An agency can reach almost any reasonable conclusion, but it has to show its work: identify the relevant considerations, engage with the evidence, respond to significant objections, and articulate a rational connection between the facts it found and the choice it made. A decision that's actually sensible can still be struck down if the agency didn't adequately explain it, because courts review the reasoning the agency gave, not reasons a lawyer invents afterward. This is the principle from an older case, *SEC v. Chenery*, that an agency's action must be judged on the basis the agency actually stated, not on some post-hoc rationalization. If the agency's stated reasoning doesn't hold up, the fact that a good reason might have existed won't save the decision.

Changing course. A recurring question is what happens when an agency changes its position, adopting a new rule that reverses an old one. Agencies are allowed to change their minds; a new administration can pursue different policies than its predecessor. But the Court has held that an agency changing course has to acknowledge that it's changing course and provide a reasoned explanation for the change. In *FCC v. Fox Television Stations* in 2009, the Court held that an agency reversing a prior policy doesn't need to prove the new policy is better than the old one, but it does have to display awareness that it's changing position and give good reasons for the new approach. It can't pretend nothing changed. And in *Encino Motorcars, LLC v. Navarro* in 2016, the Court reinforced that when an agency reverses a longstanding position on which people have relied, it owes a more detailed justification. The reliance interests people built up under the old rule are part of what the agency has to weigh and explain.

Two recent applications. Arbitrary and capricious review has decided some prominent recent cases, and two show how the standard operates when agencies get caught giving bad reasons. In *Department of Commerce v. New York* in 2019, the Court reviewed the decision to add a citizenship question to the census. The Court found that the stated rationale for the decision, that the question was needed to enforce the Voting Rights Act, appeared to be pretextual, meaning it wasn't the real reason. The evidence suggested the agency had decided to add the question first and then searched for a justification. The Court held that courts aren't required to accept an explanation that's contrived, and it blocked the question. The decision showed that arbitrary and capricious review polices honesty in agency reasoning, not just its logic.

In *Department of Homeland Security v. Regents of the University of California* in 2020, the Court reviewed the rescission of the DACA program, which protected certain immigrants brought to the country as children. The Court held the rescission arbitrary and capricious because the agency had failed to consider important aspects of the problem, including the reliance interests of the people who had built their lives around the program and whether some more limited action might have been appropriate instead of full rescission. As in *State Farm*, the agency's failure to grapple with obvious considerations and alternatives doomed its decision. The rescission might have been achievable, but not the way the agency did it.

Here's a summary of the major arbitrary and capricious cases.

Case	Year	What the Agency Did	Result
Overton Park v. Volpe	1971	Approved a highway through a park	Set standard; required review of the full record
State Farm	1983	Rescinded a passive restraint rule	Struck down; ignored an obvious alternative
FCC v. Fox	2009	Reversed an indecency policy	Upheld; agency acknowledged the change and explained it
Department of Commerce v. New York	2019	Added a census citizenship question	Struck down; the stated reason was pretextual

DHS v. Regents	2020	Rescinded DACA	Struck down; ignored reliance interests and alternatives

Arbitrary and capricious review is where a great deal of the real action in judicial review takes place, precisely because it applies so broadly. Most agency decisions don't turn on a disputed question of statutory meaning; they turn on whether the agency exercised its discretion reasonably. And because the standard demands genuine engagement and honest explanation, it gives courts a meaningful way to hold agencies accountable without second-guessing their policy choices directly. An agency that does its homework, considers the evidence, weighs the alternatives, and explains its reasoning will usually survive. An agency that acts on unexplained preference, ignores obvious problems, or offers pretextual justifications will not.

Exhaustion of Administrative Remedies

Even when a person has standing and a valid objection to what an agency did, they often can't run straight to court. A cluster of doctrines governs the timing of judicial review, requiring challengers to wait until the right moment before a court will hear them. The main one is **exhaustion of administrative remedies**, which holds that a party generally must complete the agency's own review process before seeking review in court.

The logic of exhaustion is practical. If an agency provides an internal appeal or review procedure, a party unhappy with a decision usually has to use it before going to a judge. This gives the agency a chance to correct its own errors, applies the agency's expertise to the problem first, and often resolves the dispute without judicial involvement at all. It also produces a complete administrative record for the court to review if the case does eventually reach one, and it prevents parties from interrupting agency proceedings by running to court over every intermediate step. Requiring exhaustion keeps the courts from getting drawn into disputes the agency might have fixed on its own.

Exhaustion isn't absolute, though, and courts recognize exceptions. A party might be excused from exhausting when the administrative remedy would be inadequate or futile, when pursuing it would cause irreparable harm, or when the agency clearly lacks authority to grant the relief sought. There's also a wrinkle specific to the APA. In *Darby v. Cisneros* in 1993, the Court held that when review is sought under the APA, a party isn't required to exhaust administrative appeals unless a statute or an agency rule specifically requires it. So exhaustion requirements come in different strengths depending on whether they're imposed by statute, by agency rule, or left to judicial discretion, and the source of the requirement affects how strictly it applies.

Two related doctrines govern timing alongside exhaustion, and they're worth distinguishing.

Ripeness asks whether a dispute has matured enough to be fit for judicial decision. A challenge brought too early, before the agency action has any concrete effect on the plaintiff, may be dismissed as unripe. The leading case is *Abbott Laboratories v. Gardner* in 1967, which set out a test weighing the fitness of the issues for judicial decision against the hardship to the parties of withholding review. If the issue is purely legal and the regulation has an immediate, direct impact on the party, the challenge may be ripe even before enforcement; if the impact is speculative or contingent on future events, it may not be.

Finality asks whether the agency has actually completed its decision-making. Under the APA, courts review "final agency action," meaning the agency must have arrived at a definitive position that determines rights or obligations, not a tentative or interlocutory step. The test from *Bennett v. Spear* in 1997 asks whether the action marks the consummation of the agency's decision-making process and whether legal consequences flow from it. A party can't sue over a preliminary agency step that hasn't yet become the agency's last word.

Doctrine	Question	Effect
Exhaustion	Has the party completed the agency's internal process?	Must usually finish agency review first
Ripeness	Is the dispute mature enough to decide?	Premature challenges are dismissed
Finality	Has the agency reached its definitive decision?	Only final action is reviewable

Together, these timing doctrines channel challenges to the right moment. They keep courts from intervening in agency matters prematurely, before the agency has finished its work and before the dispute has taken concrete shape. For a person aggrieved by an agency, the practical lesson is that having a good argument isn't always enough; you have to bring it at the right time, through the right channel, after the agency has had its full opportunity to act. Miss the timing, and the courthouse door stays closed until the moment is right, no matter how strong the underlying complaint.

Discussion Question

For forty years, Chevron told judges to step back and let expert agencies resolve the ambiguities in the statutes they administer, on the theory that agencies know their subjects better than courts do and answer to the voters in a way judges don't. *Loper Bright* rejected that bargain and handed the final word back to the courts. Both positions claim to serve the rule of law: one by trusting accountable experts to fill the gaps Congress leaves, the other by insisting that neutral judges, not the agencies being regulated, decide what the law means. Which arrangement actually produces more honest and reliable government, and does the answer depend on whether you trust agencies or courts more in the first place?

Chapter 7: Agency Accountability and Oversight

In 2013, a physician at the Phoenix VA hospital started noticing that veterans were dying while waiting for appointments that never came. The official records showed reasonable wait times. The reality was a system of secret lists, where the real backlog got hidden so the hospital could report numbers that looked good and staff could collect performance bonuses. Dr. Samuel Foote could have stayed quiet. Instead, he reported what he'd seen, first inside the system and then to investigators.

What happened next shows every accountability mechanism this chapter is about, firing at once. The Department of Veterans Affairs Inspector General opened an investigation and confirmed that veterans had waited months for care while the delays were concealed. Congress hauled VA officials in front of oversight committees and demanded answers under oath. Journalists filed records requests and published what they found. Within months, the Secretary of Veterans Affairs resigned, and

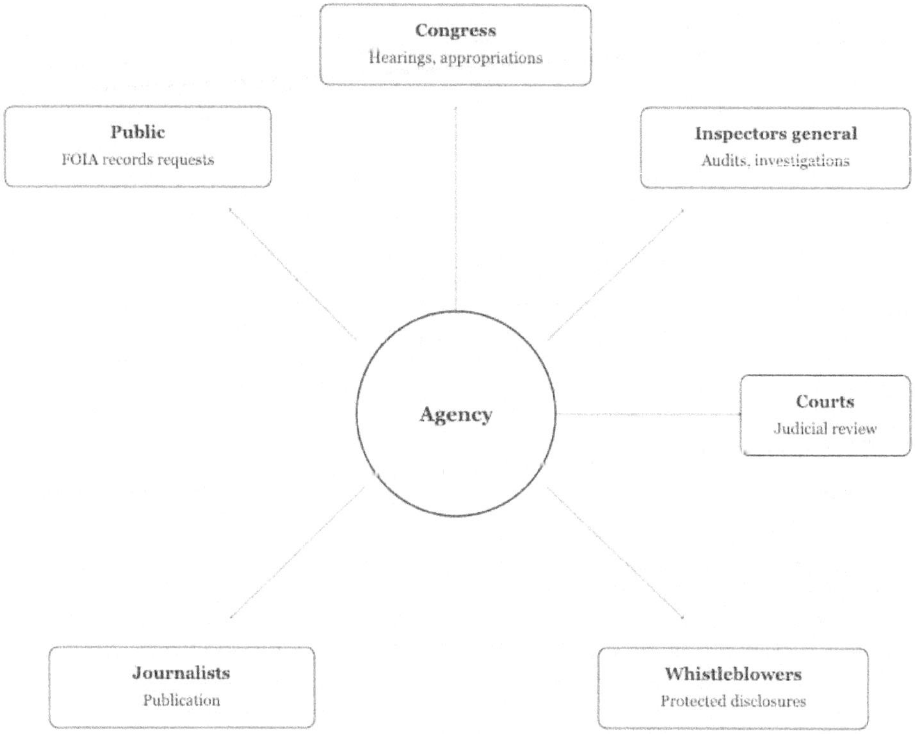

A single scandal can activate several mechanisms at once

Congress passed a law overhauling how veterans get access to care. One doctor's decision to speak, amplified by a watchdog, a legislature, and the press, brought down the head of a cabinet department and rewrote federal law.

That's the subject of this chapter. The last chapter covered how courts check agencies through judicial review. But courts aren't the only watchdogs, and they only act when someone brings a lawsuit. A whole system of oversight operates outside the courtroom, keeping agencies accountable through other means: Congress investigating and cancelling rules, internal inspectors digging for waste and abuse, the public demanding to see government records, and employees inside agencies protected when they report wrongdoing. These mechanisms answer the oldest question about government power: who watches the watchers? This chapter works through the answers.

Congressional Oversight Hearings

Congress creates agencies, funds them, and defines their powers, so it makes sense that Congress also watches over them. **Congressional oversight** is the ongoing process by which the legislature monitors how agencies carry out the laws, and the oversight hearing is its most visible tool. When a committee calls agency officials to testify, questions them about their decisions, and demands documents, it's exercising a power that keeps agencies answerable to the elected branch that created them.

Where the power comes from. The Constitution doesn't explicitly grant Congress a power to investigate, but the Supreme Court long ago recognized that the power is implied, because Congress can't legislate intelligently without the ability to gather information. The foundational case is *McGrain v. Daugherty* in 1927, which grew out of the Teapot Dome scandal. The Senate was investigating corruption at the Justice Department and tried to compel the testimony of the former attorney general's brother, who refused. The Court upheld Congress's power to compel testimony, holding that the power to investigate is an essential part of the legislative function. Congress needs facts to make laws, and it can't get those facts without the authority to require witnesses to appear and produce information. This established that congressional oversight isn't a courtesy agencies can decline; it's backed by real compulsory power.

That power isn't unlimited, though, and the Court has drawn boundaries. In *Watkins v. United States* in 1957, decided during the era of aggressive congressional investigations into subversion, the Court held that Congress's investigative power has limits. Investigations have to serve a legitimate legislative purpose, and Congress can't investigate purely to expose people's private affairs for the sake of exposure. There's no congressional power, the Court said, to inquire into private matters unrelated to a valid legislative task, and witnesses retain constitutional protections during investigations. The power to investigate exists to support legislation, not to punish or humiliate.

The tools of oversight. Congress conducts oversight through several mechanisms working together, and hearings are only the most public of them.

Tool	How It Works
Oversight hearings	Committees question agency officials, often under oath, in public sessions
Subpoenas	Committees compel testimony and the production of documents
Reports and inquiries	Committees and support agencies investigate and publish findings
Confirmation hearings	The Senate reviews nominees before they take office
The appropriations power	Congress controls agency funding and attaches conditions

The subpoena is what gives hearings their teeth. A committee can compel officials to appear and can demand documents, and refusing a valid congressional subpoena can lead to contempt of Congress. Contempt comes in a few forms. Criminal contempt involves referring the matter to a U.S. Attorney for prosecution. Civil contempt involves Congress going to court to enforce the subpoena. There's also an older, rarely used power called inherent contempt, under which Congress could theoretically detain someone itself, though it hasn't been used in modern times. In practice, subpoena fights between Congress and the executive branch often end up negotiated or litigated rather than resolved through actual contempt proceedings, but the threat shapes how agencies respond.

When oversight meets the president. Congressional subpoenas run into special complications when they seek information from the president or the White House, because the executive branch can raise claims of executive privilege and separation-of-powers concerns. The Court addressed the limits of congressional subpoena power over the president's personal records in *Trump v. Mazars USA* in 2020. Congress had subpoenaed the president's financial records from third parties, and the Court held that such subpoenas raise separation-of-powers concerns requiring courts to apply a balancing test. Courts have to weigh factors including whether the subpoena is necessary to a legitimate legislative purpose, whether it's no broader than reasonably necessary, and the burdens it imposes on the presidency. The decision recognized that congressional oversight of the executive is legitimate but subject to limits when it targets the president directly, reflecting the ongoing tension between the branches.

The power of the purse. The most consequential oversight tool isn't the hearing or the subpoena; it's money. Congress controls agency funding through the appropriations process, and that control is a continuous form of oversight far more powerful than any single hearing. An agency needs money to operate, and Congress decides how much it gets each year. This gives Congress leverage over everything agencies do, because an agency that ignores congressional wishes risks losing funding.

Congress uses this power in targeted ways through **appropriations riders**, provisions attached to funding bills that direct or restrict how money can be spent. A limitation rider might prohibit an agency from using any funds to implement a particular rule, effectively blocking the rule without repealing the statute behind it. Congress has used riders to stop agencies from enforcing regulations it dislikes, to prevent agencies from working on certain projects, and to impose all kinds of conditions on how appropriated money is used. Because these riders ride along on must-pass funding bills, they're a practical way for Congress to control agency behavior on a continuing basis. The appropriations power turns the annual budget into a recurring opportunity to rein agencies in, and agencies pay close attention to what their funders want.

Oversight through hearings, subpoenas, and appropriations keeps agencies tethered to Congress, but it has limits as a control mechanism. Hearings can be more about political theater than genuine fact-finding. Oversight tends to be sporadic, focused on whatever scandal or issue has captured attention, rather than systematic monitoring of everything agencies do. And divided government can turn oversight into a partisan weapon, aggressive when the opposing party controls an agency and lax when one's own party does. Still, the constant possibility of being called to testify, subpoenaed for documents, or defunded shapes how agencies operate, and that background pressure is part of what keeps them accountable to the elected branch.

The Congressional Review Act

Oversight hearings let Congress complain about agency rules, but complaining isn't the same as stopping. For most of the twentieth century, once an agency finalized a rule, Congress had no quick way to undo it short of passing a whole new law through the normal legislative process, which is slow and hard. In 1996, Congress created a faster tool.

The **Congressional Review Act**, usually called the CRA, gives Congress a streamlined procedure to overturn agency rules, and after sitting mostly unused for two decades, it suddenly became a real force.

How it works. The CRA requires agencies to submit every final rule to both houses of Congress and to the Government Accountability Office before the rule can take effect. This submission starts a clock. Congress then has a window, 60 legislative days, to pass a **joint resolution of disapproval** rejecting the rule. If both houses pass the resolution and the president signs it (or Congress overrides a veto), the rule doesn't take effect, and any rule already in effect is nullified.

What makes the CRA powerful is a procedural feature: in the Senate, a disapproval resolution can't be filibustered. Normally, most legislation needs 60 votes to overcome a filibuster and reach a final vote in the Senate. CRA resolutions are exempt from this. They need only a simple majority, and debate is limited. This is enormous, because it means the party controlling Congress can repeal agency rules without needing a supermajority, as long as it also controls or can work with the presidency.

The CRA turns rule repeal from a near-impossible legislative lift into something a bare majority can accomplish.

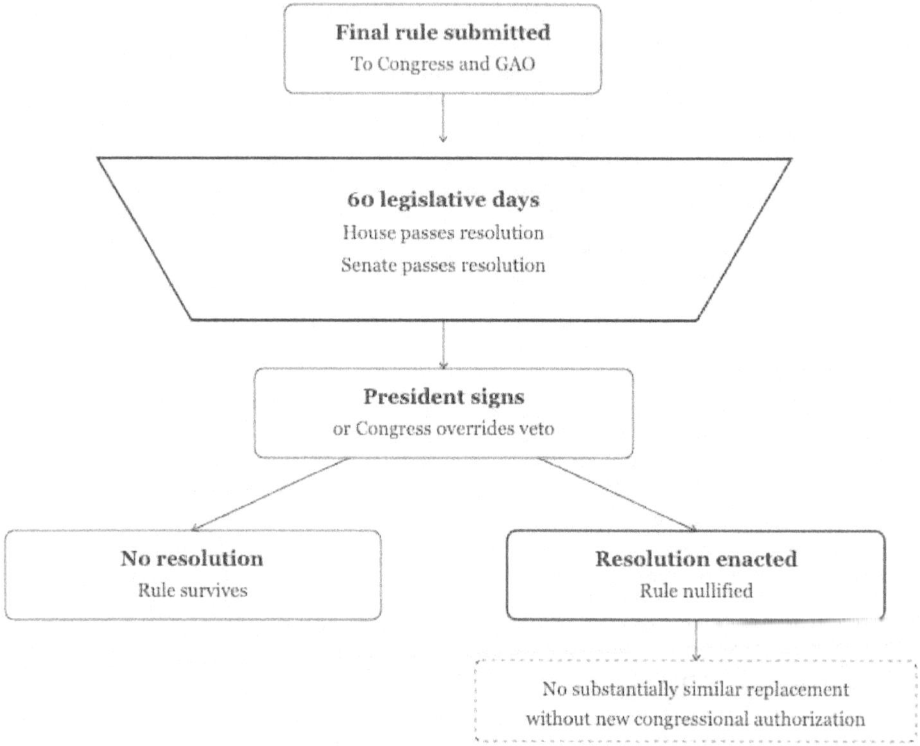

There's a sting in the tail. When Congress disapproves a rule under the CRA, the agency is barred from issuing a new rule in "substantially the same form" as the disapproved rule, unless Congress specifically authorizes it by later legislation. This provision means CRA disapproval doesn't just kill one rule; it can prevent the agency from trying again with a similar rule. The exact scope of "substantially the same" is uncertain, because it's rarely been litigated, but the provision potentially locks an agency out of a whole area of regulation, which makes CRA disapproval far more consequential than a simple veto of one rule.

Decades of dormancy, then a flood. For its first two decades, the CRA was almost a dead letter. The reason is structural: to use it, you generally need the same party to control the House, the Senate, and the presidency, because a president won't sign a resolution disapproving a rule his own administration issued. That alignment is rare, and when it exists, the rules being targeted are usually the previous administration's, finalized in the window before the new government took over. This limited the CRA to brief moments of unified government following a change in party control.

It was used successfully exactly once in its first two decades. In 2001, shortly after a change in administration, Congress used the CRA to repeal an OSHA ergonomics rule that had been finalized in the final weeks of the prior administration. That was the entire track record for years, and many observers concluded the CRA was mostly a symbolic tool that would rarely matter.

Then came 2017. After a change in party control gave one party the House, Senate, and presidency simultaneously, Congress used the CRA repeatedly to repeal rules finalized in the last stretch of the previous administration. In a span of months, Congress passed and the president signed around 16 disapproval resolutions, undoing rules on subjects ranging from environmental protection to labor to internet privacy. This burst of activity transformed the CRA from a curiosity into a demonstrated instrument of rule repeal, and it showed exactly how the tool works: it becomes potent in the window after an election flips control of both Congress and the White House, letting the new majority quickly wipe out the outgoing administration's last-minute rules.

Here's the CRA's practical profile.

Feature	Detail
Enacted	1996
What triggers it	Agencies must submit final rules to Congress and the GAO
Time window	60 legislative days to pass a disapproval resolution
Senate threshold	Simple majority; no filibuster
Effect of disapproval	Rule nullified; agency barred from "substantially similar" rule
Successful uses, 1996–2016	One (the OSHA ergonomics rule, 2001)
Successful uses in 2017	Roughly 16

The reach-back and the "rule" question. Two technical wrinkles expand the CRA's reach. The first involves timing. The CRA contains a special provision that effectively resets the clock for rules submitted near the end of a congressional session, carrying them over so a new Congress can review rules finalized in the closing months of the prior year. This "look-back" window is what lets an incoming government reach rules the outgoing administration rushed to finish, and it's why the CRA becomes relevant right after a transition.

The second wrinkle involves what counts as a "rule" subject to the CRA. The Act's definition of "rule" is broad, and it isn't limited to formal regulations that went through notice and comment. Guidance documents, bulletins, and other agency pronouncements can potentially qualify as rules under the CRA even though they never went through the rulemaking process. The Government Accountability Office issues opinions on whether particular agency actions are rules for CRA purposes, and in 2018, the GAO determined that a guidance bulletin the Consumer Financial Protection Bureau had issued on auto lending years earlier was a rule subject to the CRA. Congress then disapproved it. This showed that the CRA can reach back to agency guidance, not just formal rules, and that the GAO's role in defining "rule" can open the door to disapproving agency actions the agency never treated as rules at all. The implications are still developing, but they mean the CRA potentially covers a much wider range of agency actions than its drafters may have envisioned.

Inspector General Investigations

The oversight tools discussed so far operate from outside the agency: Congress looking in, the CRA reaching in to cancel rules. But some of the most effective oversight happens from within, through officials whose job is to police their own agencies. These are the **inspectors general**, and they occupy an unusual position: they work inside the agency they investigate, yet they're designed to operate independently of the agency's leadership. Their whole purpose is to find waste, fraud, and abuse within the government and report it, even when the findings embarrass the agency they belong to.

The design of independence. Congress created the modern inspector general system with the **Inspector General Act of 1978**, passed in the wake of government scandals that revealed a need for better internal watchdogs. The Act established inspectors general in agencies across the government, each running an office dedicated to auditing agency programs and investigating misconduct. The genius of the design is a structure meant to keep IGs independent enough to investigate honestly while keeping them close enough to know the agency well.

Several features protect that independence. In the larger agencies, the inspector general is appointed by the president and confirmed by the Senate, which gives the office a stature independent of the agency head. IGs have their own staff, their own budgets, and the authority to conduct audits and investigations without the agency's permission. They can issue subpoenas for documents in the course of their investigations. And they're supposed to be selected based on their ability and integrity rather than political considerations, so the office isn't just a tool of whoever runs the agency.

Dual reporting. The most important structural feature is that inspectors general report in two directions at once. An IG reports to the head of the agency, keeping agency leadership informed of problems, but also reports directly to Congress, which means the IG can't be silenced by the agency. This dual reporting is what makes the system work. If an IG uncovers wrongdoing that the agency head would prefer to bury, the IG can take the findings straight to Congress and the public. The obligation runs to both, so the agency can't stand between the IG and the legislature.

A central mechanism of this reporting is the semiannual report. Inspectors general are required to issue reports twice a year summarizing their findings, the problems they've identified, the money they've recovered or saved, and the status of their recommendations. These reports go to Congress and become public, creating a regular, visible record of what's going wrong inside agencies and what's being done about it. The semiannual report keeps IG oversight continuous rather than sporadic, and it produces a paper trail that Congress and the press can use.

Here's what protects and empowers an inspector general.

Feature	Purpose
Presidential appointment (larger agencies)	Independent stature above the agency head
Own budget and staff	Freedom to investigate without agency control
Subpoena authority	Power to compel documents in investigations
Dual reporting to agency head and Congress	Prevents the agency from suppressing findings
Semiannual reports	Continuous, public accountability
Removal notification requirement	Protects the IG from quiet firing

Protection from removal. Inspectors general aren't fully protected from removal, but they have a safeguard designed to make firing them politically costly. Under the law, the president can remove a presidentially appointed inspector general, but must notify Congress of the reasons at least 30 days before the removal takes effect. This notification requirement, strengthened over the years, means an IG can't simply be fired quietly. The advance notice and the requirement to give reasons expose the removal to congressional and public scrutiny, which creates a check on using removal to get rid of an IG who's investigating something inconvenient. The protection isn't absolute, and the removal of inspectors general has become contentious at various points, but the notification requirement is meant to ensure that firing a watchdog can't happen in the dark.

Coordination and impact. The inspector general system has grown into a coordinated network. The **Council of the Inspectors General on Integrity and Efficiency**, established by legislation in 2008, brings the inspectors general together to coordinate their work, share practices, and handle investigations that cross agency lines. This council gives the IG community a collective structure and a way to maintain standards across the many individual offices.

The practical output of inspectors general is substantial. IG investigations regularly uncover fraud in government programs, waste in agency spending, and misconduct by officials, and their audits recover or save large sums of money each year. High-profile IG reports have exposed serious problems, prompted the discipline or removal of officials, and driven changes in agency practices. During the COVID-19 pandemic, Congress created a special oversight structure drawing on the inspector general system to monitor the enormous sums being spent on pandemic relief, reflecting how the IG model gets deployed when the government spends money fast and the risk of fraud runs high. The inspector general system represents a bet that the most effective oversight often comes from watchdogs embedded inside agencies, close enough to know where the problems are but independent enough to expose them.

Freedom of Information Act Requests

The oversight mechanisms so far all operate through official channels: Congress, the CRA, inspectors general. But the most democratic form of accountability puts the tool directly in the hands of ordinary people. The **Freedom of Information Act**, known as FOIA, gives any person the right to request records from federal agencies, and it rests on a simple principle: the government's records belong to the public, and people are entitled to see what their government is doing. FOIA is how journalists, researchers, advocacy groups, businesses, and individual citizens pry information out of agencies that might prefer to keep it hidden.

The presumption of disclosure. Enacted in 1966, FOIA establishes a default rule that agencies must disclose their records when someone requests them. The burden is on the government to justify withholding, not on the requester to justify getting the records. Anyone can file a FOIA request, and, importantly, a requester doesn't have to give a reason or explain why they want the records. The information belongs to the public, so the public doesn't have to earn access to it. This presumption of openness is the foundation of the whole statute, and it flips the usual assumption that government information is private unless released.

The scope is broad. FOIA covers records held by federal executive branch agencies, including the departments, independent agencies, and government corporations. It doesn't cover Congress, the federal courts, or the president's personal staff, and it applies only to existing records, not to questions the requester wants answered or records the agency would have to create. But within its scope, it reaches an enormous range of government documents: reports, emails, memos, data, contracts, and more.

The nine exemptions. FOIA's presumption of disclosure isn't absolute. The statute contains nine exemptions, categories of information agencies can withhold. These exemptions are the heart of FOIA litigation, because most disputes come down to whether requested records fall within an exemption. Understanding them gives you the map of what the government can keep secret.

Exemption	What It Protects
1	Classified national security and foreign policy information
2	Internal agency personnel rules and practices

3	Information other statutes specifically exempt from disclosure
4	Trade secrets and confidential commercial or financial information
5	Privileged internal agency memos (deliberative process, attorney-client, work product)
6	Personnel, medical, and similar files where disclosure would invade personal privacy
7	Law enforcement records, where disclosure would cause specified harms
8	Records concerning the regulation of financial institutions
9	Geological and geophysical information about wells

Some of these exemptions generate far more litigation than others. **Exemption 5**, covering privileged internal communications, is heavily used and heavily fought over, because it includes the deliberative process privilege, which protects the give-and-take of agency decision-making, the drafts, recommendations, and internal debates that precede a final decision. Agencies invoke it to keep their internal deliberations private, and requesters challenge it to see how decisions were really made. The Supreme Court addressed its scope in *U.S. Fish and Wildlife Service v. Sierra Club* in 2021, holding that draft biological opinions that reflected preliminary agency views were protected as deliberative, even though they were near-final, because they didn't represent the agency's last word. The decision reinforced that the deliberative process privilege shields the internal path to a decision, not just early brainstorming.

Exemption 4, covering confidential commercial information, matters enormously to businesses. Companies submit sensitive information to agencies all the time, as part of regulatory filings, contract bids, and reporting requirements, and they don't want competitors getting it through FOIA. For years, courts limited this exemption to information whose disclosure would cause competitive harm. The Supreme Court changed that in *Food Marketing Institute v. Argus Leader Media* in 2019, holding that commercial information is "confidential" under Exemption 4 whenever it's customarily kept private by the party submitting it and provided to the government under an assurance of privacy. This broadened the exemption, making it easier for businesses to keep their submitted information secret and harder for requesters to get it. The decision was a win for businesses and a setback for transparency advocates, and it reshaped how Exemption 4 operates.

How the process works. Filing a FOIA request is straightforward in principle. A requester submits a written request to the relevant agency describing the records sought. The agency is supposed to respond within 20 business days, though in practice agencies routinely blow past this deadline, and backlogs of unanswered requests are a chronic problem. If the agency withholds records, it has to identify which exemption applies, and the requester can appeal within the agency and then sue in federal court.

Fees are part of the process, and they vary by who's asking. FOIA sorts requesters into categories that determine what they pay. Commercial requesters, seeking information for business purposes, pay the most, covering search, review, and duplication costs. Journalists, educational institutions, and noncommercial scientific researchers pay less, typically only duplication costs, because their requests serve the public interest in information. Other requesters fall in between. The statute also provides for fee waivers when disclosure would primarily benefit the public rather than the requester's private interest, which helps ensure that cost doesn't block requests made in the public interest.

FOIA in court. When an agency refuses to disclose records, the requester can sue, and FOIA litigation has developed its own procedures. Courts review the agency's withholding decisions without deference to the agency, and the agency bears the burden of proving that an exemption applies. To handle the practical problem of a court reviewing documents it can't see because they're the very records in dispute, courts use what's called a **Vaughn index**, from *Vaughn v. Rosen* in 1973. The agency has to provide a detailed index describing each withheld document and explaining why each exemption applies, so the court and the requester can evaluate the claims without the court having to examine every document in secret. This mechanism lets FOIA litigation function despite the built-in difficulty that the requester is fighting to see records they haven't been allowed to see.

FOIA also produces an unusual kind of lawsuit: the **reverse-FOIA suit**. This happens when a business that submitted information to an agency sues to *stop* the agency from releasing it in response to someone else's FOIA request. The company argues that its information falls within an exemption, usually Exemption 4, and shouldn't be disclosed. The Supreme Court addressed this in *Chrysler Corp. v. Brown* in 1979, establishing how such suits proceed. Reverse-FOIA litigation reflects the competing interests FOIA creates: requesters wanting disclosure and submitters wanting secrecy, both fighting over the same records.

Strengthening and limiting FOIA. Congress has amended FOIA repeatedly, generally to strengthen it. The **FOIA Improvement Act of 2016** made several changes designed to push agencies toward more disclosure. It codified a "foreseeable harm" standard, meaning that for the discretionary exemptions, an agency can withhold records only if it reasonably foresees that disclosure would actually harm an interest the exemption protects, rather than withholding just because it technically could. This raised the bar for withholding. The 2016 law also placed a 25-year limit on the deliberative process privilege under Exemption 5, so that internal deliberations become disclosable after a quarter century, and it required agencies to make frequently requested records available proactively. These reforms reflect a continuing push to make the presumption of disclosure real rather than nominal.

A companion statute extends the transparency principle to agency meetings. The **Government in the Sunshine Act** of 1976 requires multimember agencies, the commissions and boards, to hold their meetings open to the public, so that the deliberations of bodies like the SEC and the FCC happen in public view rather than behind closed doors. Like FOIA, it contains exemptions allowing closed sessions for sensitive matters, but the default is openness. Together, FOIA and the Sunshine Act embody the idea that a democratic government should conduct its business where the people can see it, giving the public tools to monitor agencies directly rather than relying solely on Congress or the courts.

FOIA's real-world impact is hard to overstate. Journalists have used it to expose government misconduct, uncover safety problems, and reveal what officials were doing behind closed doors. Researchers use it to study how government works. Advocacy groups use it to hold agencies to account and to gather evidence for litigation and public campaigns. The statute is imperfect, hampered by delays, backlogs, and broad exemptions, and requesters often wait months or years and litigate to get what they're entitled to. But it remains the primary way ordinary people can find out what their government is actually doing, and that makes it one of the most important accountability tools in the entire system.

Whistleblower Protections in Agencies

The Phoenix VA scandal that opened this chapter came to light because an insider spoke up. That pattern repeats throughout the history of government accountability: some of the most serious wrongdoing gets exposed not by outside investigators but by employees who see it firsthand and decide to report it. These people are whistleblowers, and because reporting your own employer's misconduct is a good way to get fired, the law protects them. **Whistleblower protections** shield government employees who disclose wrongdoing from retaliation, on the theory that people won't come forward if doing so ends their careers.

The framework. The main protections for federal employees come from the **Whistleblower Protection Act of 1989**, which built on earlier civil service reforms. The Act prohibits agencies from retaliating against employees who make protected disclosures, and it created a system for enforcing that prohibition. The system runs through two bodies. The **Office of Special Counsel** is an independent agency that investigates whistleblower complaints and can pursue corrective action on the employee's behalf. The **Merit Systems Protection Board** is a body that adjudicates disputes, including whistleblower retaliation claims, and can order remedies. Together, they give a retaliated-against employee somewhere to turn other than the agency that punished them.

What counts as a protected disclosure. Not every complaint an employee makes is protected; the law covers disclosures of specific kinds of wrongdoing. An employee is protected when they disclose information they reasonably believe shows a violation of law, rule, or regulation; gross mismanagement; a gross waste of funds; an abuse of authority; or a substantial and specific danger to public health or safety. The "reasonable belief" standard matters: the employee doesn't have to be proven right in the end, only to have reasonably believed the wrongdoing was occurring based on what they knew. This protects employees who report in good faith even if an investigation ultimately doesn't confirm the problem, because requiring certainty would deter people from reporting anything they couldn't prove.

Here's what the framework protects against and how.

Element	Detail
Protected disclosures	Violations of law, gross mismanagement, gross waste, abuse of authority, dangers to health or safety
Standard	The employee's reasonable belief, not proven fact
Prohibited retaliation	Firing, demotion, reassignment, and other adverse personnel actions
Office of Special Counsel	Investigates complaints, seeks corrective action
Merit Systems Protection Board	Adjudicates claims, orders remedies

The retaliation the law forbids covers the range of ways an agency can punish an employee: firing, demoting, reassigning to an undesirable position, denying a promotion, cutting responsibilities, or otherwise making the person's working life worse because they blew the whistle. When an employee shows that their protected disclosure was a contributing factor in an adverse personnel action, the burden shifts to the agency to prove it would have taken the same action anyway for legitimate reasons. This burden-shifting framework is meant to make retaliation claims winnable, because proving an employer's true motive is hard, and placing part of the burden on the agency helps level the field.

Closing the loopholes. The Whistleblower Protection Act didn't work as well as intended at first, partly because courts interpreted its protections narrowly, leaving gaps that let agencies retaliate in ways the law hadn't clearly covered.

Congress responded with the **Whistleblower Protection Enhancement Act of 2012**, which strengthened and clarified the protections. It closed loopholes that had developed in the case law, expanded the categories of protected disclosures, and made clear that certain disclosures courts had excluded were in fact protected. The 2012 law reflected a recognition that the original protections had been weakened over time and needed reinforcement to actually shield the people they were meant to protect.

The gaps that remain. Whistleblower protection isn't uniform across the government, and some areas fall outside the main framework. Employees in the intelligence community and in national security positions operate under different rules, because disclosing classified information raises concerns that ordinary whistleblowing doesn't. These employees have their own channels for reporting wrongdoing, designed to let them raise concerns through secure internal routes rather than public disclosure, and the protections available to them differ from those covering the general federal workforce. This creates a persistent tension: the areas of government that operate in the most secrecy, and where oversight is hardest, are also where whistleblower protections are weakest, which means the wrongdoing hardest to detect from outside is also the hardest for insiders to report safely.

A different model: paying whistleblowers. Beyond protecting employees from retaliation, some laws take a more aggressive approach and actively reward whistleblowers with money. The **False Claims Act** contains what are called qui tam provisions, which let private individuals sue on behalf of the government to recover funds lost to fraud, typically fraud by government contractors. A whistleblower who brings a successful qui tam suit, known as a relator, receives a share of the money the government recovers, which can be substantial. This creates a financial incentive to expose fraud against the government, turning private parties into enforcers. The False Claims Act has recovered enormous sums from contractors who defrauded the government, and its reward structure has proven effective at bringing fraud to light. Similar reward-based whistleblower programs exist in other areas, such as the SEC's program that pays people who report securities violations. These programs reflect a different theory of whistleblowing: rather than merely shielding people who come forward, they pay them, betting that financial rewards will surface wrongdoing that protection alone wouldn't.

The various whistleblower mechanisms, taken together, recognize a basic truth about government accountability: outside watchdogs can only see so much, and the people best positioned to spot wrongdoing are often the ones inside the agency watching it happen. Congressional oversight, inspectors general, and public records requests all depend, to some degree, on someone knowing where to look, and whistleblowers are frequently the ones who point the way. Protecting them, and sometimes rewarding them, is how the system tries to make sure that the people who see wrongdoing have a safe path to report it rather than a strong reason to stay silent. When those protections work, an insider's disclosure can set every other accountability mechanism in motion, which is exactly what happened when one doctor decided the secret waiting lists were something the public needed to know about.

Discussion Question

Every accountability mechanism in this chapter depends on someone with the will to use it: a legislator willing to hold a hearing, an inspector general willing to expose their own agency, a journalist willing to file and litigate a records request, an employee willing to risk their career by speaking up. The laws create the tools, but they can't create the courage or the political will to wield them. Given that, how much of government accountability really rests on formal legal structures, and how much rests on the character of the individuals inside and around these institutions? If the structures stay intact but the will to use them fades, would the protections on paper mean anything at all?

Chapter 8: Specialized Regulatory Domains

Everything in this book so far has been about the general machinery: how agencies get power, how they write rules, how they decide cases, how courts and Congress keep them in check. But that machinery doesn't run in the abstract. It runs inside specific agencies regulating specific problems, and the same set of tools produces strikingly different results depending on the subject. An agency protecting rivers behaves differently from one policing stock fraud, which behaves differently from one refereeing fights between unions and employers.

This chapter looks at three domains up close to show the framework in action. Each uses the powers described in earlier chapters, rulemaking, adjudication, enforcement, investigation, but each has developed its own character, shaped by the problem it handles and the statutes Congress wrote for it. Seeing how environmental, financial, and labor regulation actually work turns the general principles into something concrete, and it reveals how much the details vary even when the underlying legal structure is the same.

Environmental Regulation and the EPA

The Environmental Protection Agency is the closest thing American government has to a model of the modern regulatory agency, and it's worth understanding in depth because so much of what people picture when they think of federal regulation comes from how the EPA operates. Created in 1970 by an executive reorganization under President Nixon, the EPA pulled together environmental responsibilities that had been scattered across the government into a single agency. It doesn't run on one statute; it administers a whole collection of them, each targeting a different environmental problem, and together they give the agency authority over air, water, waste, chemicals, and contaminated land.

A statute for each problem. The breadth of the EPA's mandate comes from the number of major laws it administers. Rather than one comprehensive environmental code, Congress passed separate statutes over the years, each addressing a distinct concern.

Statute	Year	What It Regulates
Clean Air Act	1970 (major amendments 1990)	Air pollution and emissions
Clean Water Act	1972	Discharges into surface waters

Safe Drinking Water Act	1974	Contaminants in public drinking water
Resource Conservation and Recovery Act	1976	Hazardous and solid waste handling
Toxic Substances Control Act	1976	Industrial chemicals
Comprehensive Environmental Response, Compensation, and Liability Act	1980	Cleanup of contaminated sites (Superfund)

Each of these works differently. The Clean Air Act directs the EPA to set national standards for common pollutants, called National Ambient Air Quality Standards, which define how clean the outdoor air has to be for pollutants like ozone, particulate matter, and lead. The Clean Water Act, through the permit system discussed earlier in this book, controls what facilities can discharge into the nation's waters. The waste and cleanup laws take yet another approach, regulating how hazardous materials are handled and imposing liability for cleaning up contamination. The chemical law requires review of industrial chemicals. The agency's job is to make all of these operate, which means it has to master a range of scientific and technical problems that have little in common except that they all involve the environment.

Cooperative federalism. One feature runs through most of environmental regulation and shapes how the EPA actually functions day to day: it rarely does the frontline work itself. Instead, most major environmental programs use a model in which the federal government sets minimum standards and the states carry out the programs. The EPA establishes the national baseline, and states adopt their own programs that meet or exceed that baseline, subject to EPA approval. Once a state's program is approved, the state issues the permits, conducts the inspections, and handles most of the enforcement, with the EPA overseeing and stepping in when a state falls short.

This arrangement means environmental regulation is a partnership. A factory seeking a discharge permit usually deals with a state environmental agency, not the EPA directly, even though the standards trace back to federal law. The EPA sets the floor and supervises; the states run the machinery. This division lets the federal government ensure a national minimum level of protection while letting states tailor their programs and do the hands-on work. It also creates ongoing negotiation between the EPA and the states over how programs are run, and it means the intensity of environmental enforcement can vary from state to state depending on how each state administers its delegated program.

The permitting backbone. Much of environmental regulation operates through permits, translating broad statutory standards into specific obligations for individual facilities. A power plant, a factory, or a wastewater treatment plant operates under permits that spell out exactly what it can emit or discharge, what it has to monitor, and what it has to report. The permit is where abstract standards become concrete commands for a particular operation. This makes permitting the practical center of gravity for regulated businesses, because the permit, not the underlying statute, is what governs their daily operations, and fighting over permit conditions is often where the real regulatory action happens.

The cost question and the courts. Environmental regulation raises a persistent tension between protecting the environment and the cost of doing so, and how much the EPA can or must weigh costs has produced significant litigation. Different environmental statutes treat costs differently. Some direct the agency to set standards based purely on public health, without regard to cost, while others require or permit cost considerations. This creates hard interpretive questions about when the EPA has to consider costs and when it can't.

The stakes of these questions show up in major Supreme Court decisions. In *Michigan v. EPA* in 2015, the Court held that the EPA had unreasonably failed to consider costs when deciding whether to regulate power plant emissions of mercury and other toxics, ruling that it was arbitrary to ignore cost entirely at the threshold stage where the statute made regulation contingent on it being "appropriate." The decision reflected the arbitrary and capricious principles from earlier in this book, applied to the specific question of when cost has to enter the analysis.

More recently, the EPA has been at the center of two decisions that reshaped its authority. In *West Virginia v. EPA* in 2022, the Court applied the major questions doctrine (which Chapter 9 covers in detail) to strike down the EPA's attempt to regulate carbon emissions from power plants by pushing a broad shift in how electricity is generated. The Court held that a transformation of the power sector this sweeping required clear congressional authorization the statute didn't provide. Then in *Sackett v. EPA* in 2023, the Court narrowed the reach of the Clean Water Act by limiting what counts as "waters of the United States," holding that federal jurisdiction over wetlands requires a continuous surface connection to a covered body of water. This significantly cut back the agency's authority over wetlands, an area that had been contested for decades. Both decisions constrained the EPA and reflected the broader judicial skepticism toward expansive agency power that runs through the current era.

The EPA illustrates how a single agency handles enormous scientific and technical complexity across many programs, operates through partnership with the states, translates broad mandates into facility-specific permits, and constantly navigates the tension between environmental protection and economic cost, all while its authority gets tested and trimmed by the courts.

Financial Regulation and the SEC

Financial regulation approaches its subject from a completely different angle than environmental regulation, and the contrast is instructive. Where the EPA sets substantive standards for how clean the air and water must be, the Securities and Exchange Commission mostly doesn't tell companies whether their investments are good or bad. It tells them what they have to disclose. This disclosure-based philosophy is the defining feature of federal securities regulation, and understanding it explains why the SEC operates the way it does.

Disclosure, not merit. The SEC was created in 1934, in the aftermath of the 1929 stock market crash and the Depression that followed, when public confidence in the securities markets had collapsed. The approach Congress adopted rested on a specific idea: rather than having the government judge which investments are sound, require companies to tell investors the truth about themselves and let investors decide. The theory is that markets work best when everyone has accurate information, and that fraud and manipulation, not bad investments, are what the government should prevent. This is called disclosure-based regulation, and it contrasts with what's called merit regulation, where a regulator actually evaluates whether an investment is good enough to be sold.

Federal securities law generally doesn't do merit review. The SEC doesn't bless a stock offering as a good investment or reject it as a bad one; it makes sure the company disclosed the relevant risks and financial facts, and then the market sorts out the rest. A company can sell shares in a risky, money-losing venture, as long as it honestly discloses that it's a risky, money-losing venture. This philosophy shapes everything the SEC does, because its main job becomes ensuring accurate and complete disclosure rather than passing judgment on the underlying merits. (Some state securities laws, the old "blue sky" laws that predate federal regulation, historically did use merit review, which is one way state and federal approaches diverged.)

The disclosure system in practice. The disclosure philosophy runs on two statutes working together. The Securities Act of 1933 governs the initial sale of securities, requiring companies offering securities to the public to register them and provide detailed disclosures in a document investors can review before buying. The Securities Exchange Act of 1934, which created the SEC, governs the ongoing life of publicly traded companies, requiring them to file regular reports so that current information stays available to the market.

Those ongoing reports are the heart of the system, and they have familiar names.

Filing	What It Contains	Timing
Form 10-K	Comprehensive annual report with audited financials	Yearly
Form 10-Q	Quarterly financial update, unaudited	Each quarter
Form 8-K	Report of significant events as they happen	Within days of the event

Through these filings, public companies keep the market informed about their finances and material developments. The 10-K gives a full annual picture, the 10-Q provides quarterly updates, and the 8-K reports major events like executive changes, mergers, or bankruptcies as they occur. This continuous flow of standardized, mandatory disclosure is what lets investors and analysts evaluate companies on current information, and producing it accurately is a major part of what it means to be a public company.

Policing fraud. While the SEC generally doesn't judge investment merit, it aggressively polices fraud, and its anti-fraud authority is where much of its enforcement power lives. The central tool is Rule 10b-5, a rule the SEC adopted under the 1934 Act that broadly prohibits fraud and deception in connection with the purchase or sale of securities. This rule is the basis for a huge amount of securities enforcement, covering misrepresentations, omissions of material facts, and schemes to defraud investors. When a company lies in its disclosures, or when someone manipulates a stock, Rule 10b-5 is typically what they've violated.

Insider trading enforcement flows from this anti-fraud authority. Trading on material, nonpublic information in breach of a duty is treated as a form of securities fraud, and the SEC pursues insider trading cases as part of keeping the markets honest. The law of insider trading has developed largely through enforcement actions and court decisions rather than detailed statutes, which makes it an area shaped heavily by how the SEC and the courts have interpreted the general anti-fraud prohibition over time.

A crowded field. Unlike environmental regulation, where the EPA is the dominant federal player, financial regulation is divided among many agencies, and the SEC is only one piece of a complicated structure. The financial system is regulated by a patchwork of federal bodies, each covering a different slice.

The Federal Reserve oversees the banking system and monetary policy. The Office of the Comptroller of the Currency regulates national banks. The Federal Deposit Insurance Corporation insures bank deposits and regulates certain banks. The Commodity Futures Trading Commission regulates derivatives and futures markets, a domain separate from the securities the SEC oversees. The Consumer Financial Protection Bureau, created after the 2008 crisis, focuses on consumer financial products. And the SEC itself works alongside a self-regulatory organization, the Financial Industry Regulatory Authority, which oversees brokers and dealers under SEC supervision. This fragmentation means financial regulation involves overlapping jurisdictions and coordination among agencies, and it stands in sharp contrast to the more consolidated structure of environmental regulation.

Regulation after crisis. Financial regulation tends to expand after financial disasters, and the pattern repeats across history. The SEC itself was born from the 1929 crash. The most recent major expansion came after the 2008 financial crisis, when Congress passed the Dodd-Frank Wall Street Reform and Consumer Protection Act in 2010. Dodd-Frank was a sweeping response to the crisis, creating the Consumer Financial Protection Bureau, expanding regulation of derivatives and large financial institutions, adding new requirements for financial firms, and directing agencies to write dozens of new rules. It generated an enormous amount of rulemaking as agencies implemented its provisions, and it reshaped the financial regulatory structure in ways that are still being worked out. Dodd-Frank shows how a crisis drives regulatory growth, and how a single statute can hand agencies mandates that take years to fully carry out. The SEC has also faced newer challenges the disclosure framework wasn't designed for, including how to regulate cryptocurrency and digital assets and whether to require companies to disclose climate-related risks, questions that test how a system built in the 1930s applies to modern financial products.

Labor and Employment Regulation

Labor and employment regulation differs from both environmental and financial regulation in a revealing way: it's spread across several agencies with distinct missions, and one of those agencies makes policy through a method the others largely avoid. Rather than a single dominant regulator, the field is divided among bodies that handle unions, workplace safety, wages, and discrimination, each shaped by different statutes and each with its own way of operating.

The major players. Four main agencies handle the bulk of federal labor and employment regulation, and knowing which does what maps the field.

Agency	Primary Statute(s)	Focus
National Labor Relations Board	National Labor Relations Act (1935)	Union organizing and collective bargaining
Occupational Safety and Health Administration	OSH Act (1970)	Workplace safety and health
Wage and Hour Division (Dept. of Labor)	Fair Labor Standards Act (1938)	Minimum wage, overtime, child labor
Equal Employment Opportunity Commission	Title VII (1964), ADA, ADEA	Employment discrimination

Each occupies its own territory. The NLRB, an independent agency, referees the relationship between unions and employers, deciding representation questions and unfair labor practice charges. OSHA, discussed earlier in this book, sets and enforces workplace safety standards. The Wage and Hour Division within the Department of Labor enforces the minimum wage, overtime pay, and child labor rules under the Fair Labor Standards Act. And the EEOC enforces the laws against employment discrimination based on characteristics like race, sex, religion, national origin, disability, and age, drawing on Title VII of the Civil Rights Act and related statutes.

Governing through cases. The most distinctive feature of labor regulation is how the NLRB makes policy, and it stands as the clearest example in all of administrative law of an agency that regulates primarily through adjudication rather than rulemaking. Most agencies write rules to set policy. The NLRB, for the most part, doesn't. It develops labor law case by case, deciding individual disputes and, through those decisions, establishing the principles that govern union-management relations.

When the Board wants to change the law, it usually does so by deciding a case differently than before, not by issuing a regulation.

The Supreme Court blessed this approach long ago in *SEC v. Chenery Corp.* in 1947, sometimes called Chenery II, which held that agencies have discretion to make policy through adjudication instead of rulemaking. That principle applies across administrative law, but the NLRB embraced it more fully than almost any other agency, building its entire body of labor doctrine through decisions rather than rules.

This method has a consequence that connects back to the executive and independent agency dynamics discussed earlier. Because the NLRB makes policy through the cases it decides, and because its members are appointed by the president with staggered terms, its interpretations of labor law tend to swing when control of the Board changes with new administrations. A Board with a majority appointed by one party may read the labor laws one way; a Board with a majority from the other party may reverse those interpretations in later cases. This produces a back-and-forth in labor law, where doctrines established under one administration get overturned under the next, all through the ordinary process of deciding cases. Labor law is therefore less stable than areas governed by entrenched regulations, because case-by-case policymaking is easier to reverse than a formal rule, and the shifting composition of the Board drives the changes.

Overlapping coverage. The division of labor among these agencies means a single workplace situation can implicate several of them at once. A worker might have a wage claim under the Fair Labor Standards Act handled by the Wage and Hour Division, a discrimination claim under Title VII handled by the EEOC, a safety complaint handled by OSHA, and a claim about union activity handled by the NLRB, all arising from the same employment. Each agency addresses its own piece under its own statute with its own procedures. This fragmentation reflects how employment law grew up in pieces over decades, with Congress adding protections one statute at a time rather than building a unified system, and it means understanding a workplace legal problem often requires figuring out which agency, or which combination of agencies, has authority over which part.

The three domains in this chapter, taken together, show how much variation the general framework of administrative law accommodates. The EPA regulates through substantive standards and permits, working in partnership with the states across many technical programs. The SEC regulates through mandatory disclosure and anti-fraud enforcement, operating within a fragmented financial regulatory structure. Labor agencies regulate through a mix of methods, with the NLRB standing out for governing through adjudication and swinging with each administration.

The same tools, rulemaking, adjudication, enforcement, and investigation, produce these different systems because each agency adapted the tools to its own problem and its own governing statutes. The framework is constant; what agencies build with it is not.

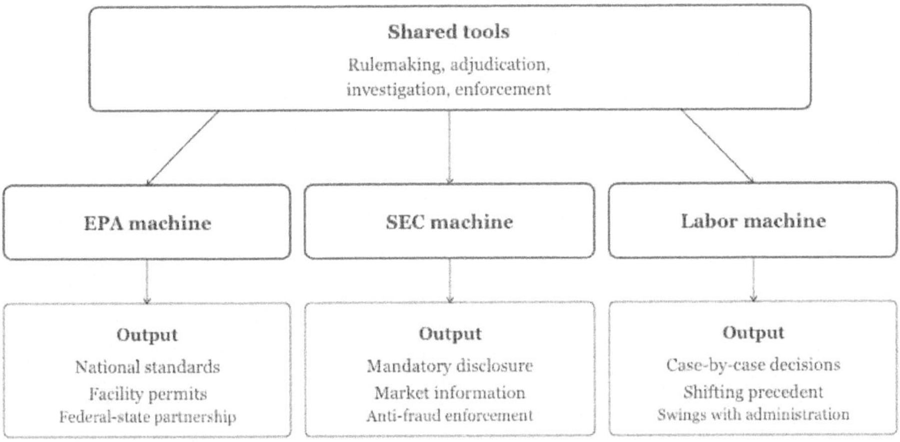

Discussion Question

These three domains solved the same basic problem, controlling private behavior in the public interest, in very different ways: the EPA by setting hard standards, the SEC by forcing disclosure and trusting the market, and the labor agencies by refereeing disputes case by case. Each approach reflects a different bet about how much the government should decide directly versus how much it should leave to informed private choice.

Looking across the three, is one model clearly better, or does the right approach depend entirely on the nature of the problem being regulated? And what does it say about American government that these three systems, built at different times to solve different problems, never got knit into anything resembling a coherent whole?

Chapter 9: Emerging Issues and the Future of Administrative Law

Between 2013 and 2015, the state of Michigan accused more than 40,000 people of unemployment fraud. It sent them demand letters, garnished their wages, seized their tax refunds, and hit them with penalties that ran to four times the amount they'd supposedly stolen. Some lost their homes. Some filed for bankruptcy. There was one problem with all of it: the accusations were mostly wrong. The state had turned the fraud determinations over to an automated system called MiDAS, and the machine was flagging people as fraudsters with an error rate that later reviews put at around 93 percent. No human looked at most of the cases before the state started collecting. The computer decided, and the government acted on what it decided.

The people who'd been falsely accused sued, and the litigation dragged on for years. But the damage was done, and the episode became a warning about what happens when an agency hands its judgment to an algorithm without keeping a human in the loop or giving people a real way to fight back.

That story points at the theme of this final chapter. Administrative law isn't a settled body of rules sitting quietly in a casebook. It's being pushed and reshaped right now by forces the framers of the Administrative Procedure Act never imagined and by a Supreme Court determined to rethink the balance of power it inherited. Someone who studied this field in 2015 would find parts of it unrecognizable today. This chapter looks at where things are heading: how artificial intelligence is entering agency decision-making, how a newly muscular doctrine is reining in agency power, how deregulation actually works, how states are experimenting ahead of the federal government, how regulation crosses borders, and what the end of Chevron means for the future. The through-line is a field in motion, with the relationship among Congress, agencies, and courts being renegotiated in real time.

Artificial Intelligence in Agency Decision-Making

Agencies process staggering volumes of decisions. The Social Security Administration handles millions of disability claims. The IRS screens hundreds of millions of tax returns. Immigration agencies review mountains of applications. Faced with this scale, agencies have turned to automation, and increasingly to artificial intelligence and machine learning, to help them cope. The technology promises speed, consistency, and the ability to spot patterns humans would miss. It also raises problems that the existing framework of administrative law wasn't built to handle, and those problems are only getting sharper as the tools get more capable.

How agencies already use it. AI in government isn't a future prospect; it's a current reality spread across many agencies. A comprehensive study of federal agency use of AI, produced for the Administrative Conference of the United States and published in 2020, found that a substantial share of federal agencies were already using machine learning and related tools for a range of tasks. Agencies use these systems to detect fraud, flagging suspicious claims or transactions for further review. They use them to prioritize enforcement, identifying which cases or facilities to investigate. They use them to support adjudication, helping sort and analyze the flood of applications and claims agencies receive. And they use them to allocate resources and predict where problems are likely to arise.

Some uses are relatively uncontroversial, like tools that help agency staff search documents or organize caseloads. Others reach into the heart of decisions that affect people's rights and benefits, and that's where the difficulty starts. When an algorithm determines how many hours of home care a disabled person receives, or flags someone for a fraud investigation, or influences whether a benefit gets approved, the machine is participating in a decision that the law surrounds with procedural protections. The question is whether those protections still work when a computer is doing part of the deciding.

The black box problem. The central legal challenge is transparency, and it connects directly to the due process principles from earlier in this book. Due process generally requires that a person affected by a government decision be able to understand the basis for it and challenge it. But many AI systems are opaque. Complex machine learning models can produce results that even their designers can't fully explain, and when agencies buy these systems from private vendors, the vendors often claim the algorithms are proprietary trade secrets that can't be disclosed. This creates a situation where a person is told the government has decided something about them, but neither they nor sometimes the agency itself can explain exactly why the algorithm reached that result.

Courts have started grappling with this. In an Idaho case, K.W. v. Armstrong, decided in the 2010s, the state used a formula to determine the budgets for Medicaid recipients receiving home-based care, and the formula slashed many people's benefits. When recipients challenged the cuts, it turned out the state couldn't adequately explain how the formula worked or why it produced the numbers it did. The court found that the process violated due process, because people couldn't meaningfully contest a decision the state itself couldn't explain. The case stands for a principle that's going to matter more and more: an agency can't hide behind a black box. If a person has a right to challenge a decision, the agency has to be able to explain the basis for it, and an unexplainable algorithm doesn't satisfy that requirement.

Bias baked in. A second problem is that AI systems can embed and amplify bias. Machine learning models learn from historical data, and if that data reflects past discrimination or skewed patterns, the model can reproduce and even magnify those patterns while wearing a veneer of mathematical objectivity. An algorithm trained on data from a system that historically treated certain groups unfairly may learn to treat them unfairly too, and because the output looks like the neutral product of a computer, the bias can be harder to spot and challenge than an obviously prejudiced human decision. This raises equal protection concerns and forces agencies to confront whether their tools are producing discriminatory results, a question that requires ongoing testing and auditing that many agencies aren't equipped to do.

Is an algorithm a rule? AI also scrambles the categories the APA is built on. When an agency adopts an algorithm that systematically determines outcomes across many cases, is that a rule that should go through notice-and-comment rulemaking? An algorithm that decides how benefits get calculated functions a lot like a rule, setting a general policy that applies to everyone in a category. But agencies have often adopted these systems as internal tools or through procurement contracts, without treating them as rules and without the public participation that rulemaking requires. This means a policy choice with broad effects can get embedded in code without the public ever getting the chance to comment on it that they'd have if the same policy were written as a regulation. Whether and when algorithmic policymaking should trigger rulemaking procedures is an unsettled question the law hasn't fully answered.

Policy in flux. The government's approach to AI has been evolving quickly, mostly through executive action, and it illustrates a pattern this book has returned to. Recent administrations have issued executive orders and guidance directing how federal agencies develop, procure, and use artificial intelligence, addressing issues like testing for bias, ensuring transparency, and maintaining human oversight of consequential decisions. And like much else set through executive orders rather than statute, the direction has shifted with changes in administration, with new leadership revising or replacing prior AI policies. This means the rules governing government

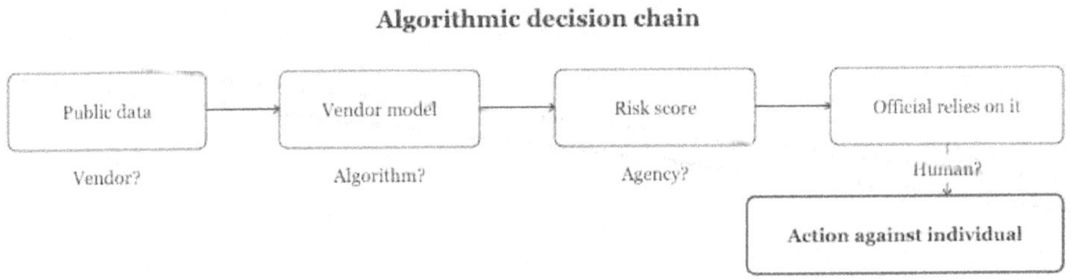

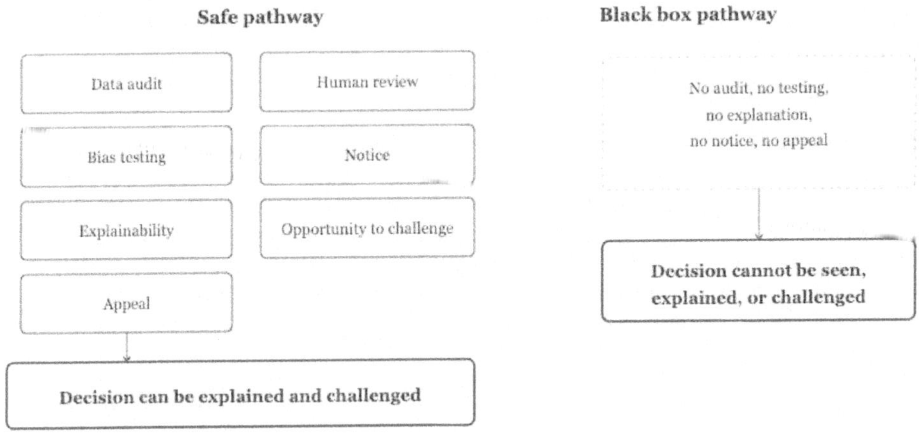

Michigan: tens of thousands of decisions, no working safeguards

use of AI are themselves unstable, changing with the political winds rather than resting on a firm statutory foundation.

The deeper issue is accountability. Administrative law is built on the premise that identifiable officials make decisions and can be held responsible for them, through the procedures, explanations, and review mechanisms this book has described. AI complicates that premise by diffusing responsibility. When a machine participates in a decision, who's accountable for the result: the agency that deployed it, the vendor that built it, the official who relied on it, or no one in particular? The Michigan fraud disaster showed what happens when this question goes unanswered, when a system makes tens of thousands of consequential decisions and the accountability structures that should have caught the errors simply weren't there. As agencies adopt more capable AI, the field will have to work out how to keep the technology within the framework of transparency, participation, and accountability that legitimizes agency power, or risk that power operating in ways no one can see, explain, or challenge.

The Major Questions Doctrine

While AI tests the framework from the outside, a doctrine developed by the Supreme Court is reshaping agency power from within the courts, and it's become one of the most consequential tools in administrative law. The **major questions doctrine** holds that when an agency claims the power to decide a question of vast economic and political significance, courts won't read a broad or ambiguous statute to grant that power unless Congress has clearly said so. It's a clear-statement rule: for the biggest questions, silence or ambiguity in the statute isn't enough, and the agency needs explicit authorization.

The logic and its target. The doctrine rests on an idea about how Congress works. When Congress means to hand an agency authority over something enormous, the reasoning goes, it does so clearly and directly, not by burying the grant in a vague phrase or an old, general provision. So when an agency discovers sweeping new power in a statute that had never been read that way before, courts should be skeptical. As the Court has put it, it expects Congress to speak clearly when it wishes to assign decisions of vast economic and political significance to an agency. The doctrine targets a specific move: an agency taking a broad but previously modest statutory authority and stretching it to justify a transformative new policy. When an agency does that, the major questions doctrine says the stretch requires clear congressional backing the agency usually can't produce.

The build-up. The doctrine didn't appear overnight; it developed over decades before it got its name. Early signs came in cases where the Court refused to let agencies find huge powers in unlikely statutory places. In *MCI Telecommunications Corp. v. AT&T* in 1994, the Court held that the FCC couldn't use its authority to "modify" rate-filing requirements to eliminate them for most carriers, because a change that big couldn't hide in a word as modest as "modify." In *FDA v. Brown & Williamson* in 2000, the tobacco case discussed earlier in this book, the Court doubted that Congress would have handed the FDA authority over an industry as economically and politically enormous as tobacco through the general language of the Food, Drug, and Cosmetic Act. In *Utility Air Regulatory Group v. EPA* in 2014, the Court rejected the EPA's attempt to rewrite specific statutory thresholds for greenhouse gas permitting, warning against agencies discovering vast power in vague language. And in *King v. Burwell* in 2015, the Court declined to apply Chevron deference to a question of deep economic and political importance under the Affordable Care Act, deciding the statutory question itself instead. Each of these planted seeds of the idea that the biggest questions get different treatment.

The COVID crystallization. The doctrine came into full force during the coronavirus pandemic, when agencies invoked emergency powers to take sweeping actions and the Court repeatedly pushed back. In *Alabama Association of Realtors v. Department of Health and Human Services* in 2021, the Court struck down a nationwide eviction moratorium the CDC had imposed to prevent the spread of COVID. The CDC claimed authority under a public health statute, but the Court held that a measure this economically significant, reaching the landlord-tenant relationships of millions of people, required clear congressional authorization the statute didn't provide. Reading the statute to grant such power, the Court said, would give the agency breathtaking authority over a huge swath of the economy based on thin statutory language.

A few months later, in *National Federation of Independent Business v. OSHA* in 2022, the Court blocked OSHA's rule requiring large employers to mandate that their workers be vaccinated or regularly tested. The Court reasoned that OSHA's authority to regulate workplace safety didn't clearly extend to a broad public health measure affecting tens of millions of workers across every industry. A mandate of that scope and significance, the Court held, needed clearer authorization than the general workplace safety statute supplied. These two decisions applied the major questions reasoning to strike down major exercises of agency power, showing how the doctrine could stop agencies even in a genuine emergency.

West Virginia names the doctrine. The case that formalized the major questions doctrine as a named doctrine, mentioned earlier in this book, was *West Virginia v. EPA* in 2022. Chief Justice Roberts, writing for the Court, used the phrase and treated it as an established principle. The case concerned the EPA's authority to regulate carbon emissions from power plants, specifically an approach that would have pushed the entire electricity sector to shift away from coal toward cleaner generation, a strategy called generation-shifting. The Court held that forcing a transformation of how the nation produces electricity was a decision of such magnitude that the EPA couldn't undertake it without clear congressional authorization, which the Clean Air Act provision the agency relied on didn't provide.

Roberts described the doctrine as applying in extraordinary cases where the history and breadth of the authority an agency asserts, combined with the economic and political significance of the action, give reason to hesitate before concluding that Congress meant to confer such power. Justice Gorsuch wrote a concurrence tying the doctrine explicitly to the separation of powers and to concerns about agencies exercising what amounts to legislative authority, connecting it to the nondelegation ideas discussed in the first chapter of this book. *West Virginia* turned a pattern of decisions into a doctrine with a name and a framework, and it signaled that the Court would use it aggressively.

Student loans and the doctrine's reach. The doctrine's power became even clearer in *Biden v. Nebraska* in 2023, which struck down a student loan forgiveness program that would have cancelled roughly 430 billion dollars in debt. The administration claimed authority under a statute allowing it to "waive or modify" loan provisions in national emergencies. The Court held that cancelling debt on this scale, affecting tens of millions of borrowers and hundreds of billions of dollars, was a quintessential major question that the statute's language didn't clearly authorize. The words "waive or modify," the Court reasoned, couldn't bear the weight of a program this transformative. The decision showed the doctrine reaching one of the largest exercises of administrative power in recent memory and reinforced that economic magnitude is central to what makes a question major.

Here's how the major recent cases line up.

Case	Year	Agency Action	Result
MCI v. AT&T	1994	FCC eliminating rate-filing for most carriers	Struck down; too big for "modify"
Brown & Williamson	2000	FDA regulating tobacco	Struck down; too significant for vague grant
UARG v. EPA	2014	EPA rewriting permit thresholds	Struck down; agency overreach
Alabama Realtors v. HHS	2021	CDC eviction moratorium	Struck down; needed clear authorization
NFIB v. OSHA	2022	OSHA vaccine-or-test mandate	Blocked; beyond clear authority
West Virginia v. EPA	2022	EPA generation-shifting for power plants	Struck down; doctrine named
Biden v. Nebraska	2023	Student loan forgiveness	Struck down; major question

The criticism. The major questions doctrine has drawn sharp criticism, much of it from within the Court itself. The central objection is that "major" has no clear definition. What makes a question major rather than ordinary? The doctrine points to economic and political significance, but almost any significant regulation has substantial economic effects and political stakes, which gives courts wide room to decide that whatever agency action they dislike happens to cross the threshold. Justice Kagan, dissenting in *West Virginia*, argued that the majority had appointed itself, rather than Congress or the expert agency, as the decision-maker on climate policy, and that the doctrine let the Court substitute its own judgment for the agency's under the guise of interpreting statutes. She made a similar argument dissenting in *Biden v. Nebraska*, contending that the Court was using the doctrine to override clear statutory text it didn't like.

There's also a tension with the Court's own commitment to textualism. Textualism says judges should follow the words Congress wrote. Critics point out that the major questions doctrine is a substantive canon that can override the ordinary meaning of the text, refusing to read a statute the way its words would naturally be read because the result would be too big. This makes the doctrine, in the eyes of its critics, a departure from textualism dressed up as interpretation, and a way for the Court to impose a small-government preference regardless of what statutes actually say. Defenders respond that the doctrine reflects a realistic understanding of how Congress delegates and protects the separation of powers by keeping the biggest decisions with the elected legislature rather than with agencies.

How it fits with the end of Chevron. The major questions doctrine works together with the overruling of Chevron, discussed in the previous chapter, to shift power from agencies to courts. Under the old regime, the major questions doctrine functioned as a carve-out from Chevron: for most questions, courts deferred to reasonable agency interpretations, but for major questions, they didn't. Now that Chevron is gone and courts interpret statutes independently across the board, the major questions doctrine remains as a distinct and even more potent tool for the biggest cases. It doesn't just deny deference; it imposes an affirmative requirement of clear congressional authorization, a higher bar than ordinary interpretation. Together, the two developments mean agencies face heightened judicial skepticism generally and a special hurdle for their most ambitious actions, and both point in the same direction: less agency power, more judicial control over what agencies can do.

Deregulation Movements and Regulatory Rollback

Regulation moves in cycles. Administrations that favor an active government expand agency rules; administrations that favor a smaller government try to cut them back. This back-and-forth, with regulation building up under some presidents and getting rolled back under others, is a permanent feature of the system. But rolling back regulation turns out to be harder than it looks, and understanding why reveals something important about how the administrative state actually works.

The tools of rollback. An administration wanting to reduce regulation has several tools, and each has limits.

Tool	How It Works	Limit
Rescinding rules	Repealing a regulation through new rulemaking	Requires notice, comment, and reasoned explanation
Congressional Review Act	Congress cancels recent rules by resolution	Needs unified government and a narrow time window

Executive orders	Directives to cut rules, cap new ones, set regulatory budgets	Can't override statutory duties
Non-enforcement	Declining to pursue violations	Can't abandon mandatory statutory obligations
Litigation posture	Not defending challenged rules; delaying effective dates	Delays and reversals are themselves reviewable

The Congressional Review Act, covered earlier in this book, is one route, and its burst of use following the change in party control demonstrated how a new government can quickly wipe out an outgoing administration's late rules. Executive orders are another. Administrations have issued orders directing agencies to cut regulations, including requirements that agencies repeal a certain number of existing rules for each new one they issue, and orders imposing "regulatory budgets" that cap the total cost of an agency's rules. These orders push agencies toward deregulation, though they can't authorize agencies to ignore duties their statutes impose.

The procedural symmetry that traps deregulation. Here's the thing that surprises people: deregulation is subject to the same procedural requirements as regulation. Rescinding a rule is itself a form of rulemaking. An agency can't simply announce that a regulation no longer applies; to repeal a rule that went through notice and comment, the agency generally has to go through notice and comment again, and it has to provide a reasoned explanation for the repeal. The arbitrary and capricious standard, discussed in the previous chapter, applies to getting rid of a rule just as it applies to making one. This principle traces directly to *State Farm*, the passive restraint case, which was itself a challenge to a rule rescission. The Court there made clear that an agency reversing course has to justify the reversal with the same care it would need to justify the original rule.

This procedural symmetry has real consequences. When one recent administration pursued an aggressive deregulatory agenda, it lost a striking share of the resulting court challenges, and it lost most of them on administrative law grounds rather than on the underlying policy. Agencies moved fast to undo rules and cut procedural corners in the process, failing to adequately explain their reversals, ignoring evidence, or skipping required steps, and courts struck the actions down for violating the APA. The same requirements that make regulation slow and cumbersome make deregulation slow and cumbersome too. An administration can't dismantle the regulatory state quickly for the same reason a prior administration couldn't build it quickly: the process demands explanation, evidence, and public participation in both directions.

The trick of delay. One tactic agencies tried was simply delaying the effective dates of rules they wanted to eliminate, postponing them indefinitely rather than formally repealing them. Courts caught on to this. They held that delaying or suspending a rule's effective date is itself a substantive action that changes the legal status quo, and therefore is itself subject to notice-and-comment requirements and reasoned-explanation demands. An agency can't evade the procedures for repealing a rule by just pressing pause on it. This closed off what looked like a shortcut and reinforced that agencies can't escape procedural obligations by relabeling what they're doing.

Non-enforcement and its limits. A subtler form of deregulation is simply declining to enforce existing rules. An administration that can't easily repeal a regulation can sometimes achieve a similar result by directing agencies not to pursue violations, letting the rule stay on the books while going unenforced. Agencies have broad discretion here, and this discretion is largely shielded from judicial review. The Supreme Court held in *Heckler v. Chaney* in 1985 that an agency's decision not to take enforcement action is presumptively unreviewable, reasoning that enforcement decisions involve balancing priorities and resources in ways courts aren't well suited to second-guess. This gives administrations significant room to soften regulation through non-enforcement without the procedural burdens of formal repeal.

But this discretion has limits. The presumption against reviewing non-enforcement isn't absolute, and it doesn't let an agency abandon a duty its statute makes mandatory. When a statute requires an agency to act, using the mandatory language discussed earlier in this book, the agency can't simply refuse to carry out that duty and call it enforcement discretion. And a blanket policy of non-enforcement that amounts to rewriting the law, rather than case-by-case exercises of discretion, can cross into reviewable territory. So non-enforcement is a real deregulatory tool, but it can't be stretched into a general power to nullify statutory obligations the agency doesn't like.

The pattern that emerges is one of constraint on deregulation as much as on regulation. The administrative state, once built, is sticky. Its rules can be changed, but changing them requires the same procedural rigor that creating them did, and administrations that ignore this reality find their deregulatory actions unwound by courts. This is a feature of the system that cuts against whoever holds power at a given moment, and it means the regulatory state tends to change gradually rather than lurching dramatically with each election, whatever an incoming administration might prefer.

State-Level Administrative Reform

The debates reshaping federal administrative law are playing out at the state level too, and in some respects the states have moved faster and further than the federal government. Every state has its own administrative law governing its own agencies, and states have served as testing grounds for reforms that are only now reaching the federal system. Watching what states have done offers a preview of where administrative law might go and shows that the impulse to rein in agencies isn't confined to Washington.

States rejecting deference first. The most striking example is deference to agency interpretations. Long before the Supreme Court overruled Chevron, a wave of states had already abandoned or curtailed the practice of deferring to their own agencies' interpretations of law. Some did it through court decisions. The Wisconsin Supreme Court, in *Tetra Tech EC, Inc. v. Wisconsin Department of Revenue* in 2018, ended the state's practice of deferring to administrative agency interpretations of statutes, holding that courts would decide legal questions independently. Other state high courts, including in Mississippi, Michigan, and elsewhere, moved in the same direction, rejecting Chevron-style deference under their own state law.

Other states did it through legislation or even constitutional amendment. Arizona enacted a statute in 2018 directing courts to decide all questions of law without deferring to agency interpretations in cases brought under the state's administrative procedure act. Florida went furthest, amending its state constitution in 2018 through a ballot measure that prohibits state courts and administrative law judges from deferring to an agency's interpretation of a statute or rule, requiring them to interpret the law independently instead. These reforms put states ahead of the federal courts, which didn't reach the same result until *Loper Bright* in 2024. The states, in effect, ran the experiment first, and their experience with independent judicial review of agency interpretations offers a glimpse of what the post-Chevron federal system may look like.

Stronger nondelegation at the state level. States have also been more willing than the federal courts to enforce the nondelegation doctrine, the principle discussed in the first chapter of this book that legislatures can't hand their lawmaking power to agencies. While the federal nondelegation doctrine has been nearly toothless since 1935, some state constitutions contain stronger separation-of-powers provisions, and some state courts apply nondelegation more actively. State courts have struck down delegations to state agencies that would almost certainly survive under the lenient federal standard, demanding that state legislatures provide more specific guidance before agencies can act. This makes state nondelegation law a live area where the doctrine actually constrains agencies, in contrast to its dormant federal counterpart, and it's part of why some observers watch state developments for signs of where a revived federal nondelegation doctrine might head.

Legislative control of major rules. A number of states have adopted mechanisms giving their legislatures direct control over major agency rules, going beyond anything that exists at the federal level. These laws, modeled on a proposal that has repeatedly been introduced but never passed in Congress, require that significant agency rules receive legislative approval before taking effect, or give legislative committees the power to block or suspend rules. Some states require that rules exceeding a certain economic threshold be approved by the legislature. This inverts the usual arrangement, in which agencies issue rules and the legislature can only override them through the difficult process of passing new legislation. Under these state laws, major rules don't take effect unless the legislature affirmatively signs off, giving elected legislators a much firmer grip on agency policymaking.

Here's a summary of the main state reform trends.

Reform	Example	Effect
Ending judicial deference	Wisconsin (court), Arizona (statute), Florida (constitution)	Courts interpret law without deferring to agencies

Stronger nondelegation	Various state courts	Delegations struck down that would survive federally
Legislative approval of major rules	Several states	Big rules need legislative sign-off to take effect

These state reforms reflect a broader current running through American law: skepticism of agency power and a desire to shift authority back toward legislatures and courts. The states, with their fifty separate systems, function as laboratories where different approaches to reining in agencies can be tried and their consequences observed. What works and what doesn't at the state level informs the national debate, and the fact that states moved on deference years before the federal courts did suggests the states will keep serving as early indicators of where administrative law is heading. For anyone trying to understand the future of the field, the states are worth watching, because they're often where the future arrives first.

International Regulatory Cooperation

Regulation increasingly refuses to stay within national borders, because the things being regulated don't. Commerce is global, financial markets are interconnected, pollution crosses boundaries, and products move around the world. This reality has pushed agencies into growing cooperation with their foreign counterparts and into international standard-setting that shapes domestic regulation in ways the traditional administrative law framework wasn't designed to handle.

Coordination across borders. Agencies increasingly work with foreign regulators and participate in international bodies that set standards adopted around the world. In banking, the Basel Committee on Banking Supervision brings together regulators from major economies to set international standards for how much capital banks must hold, and American regulators implement versions of these Basel standards domestically. In securities, the SEC participates in the International Organization of Securities Commissions, which coordinates securities regulation across countries. In aviation, the FAA works within international frameworks and negotiates agreements with foreign authorities so that aircraft and parts certified in one country can be accepted in another. These arrangements let regulation function across a global economy, avoiding a chaotic situation where every country's incompatible rules would grind international commerce to a halt.

The Brussels Effect. One of the most interesting dynamics in global regulation is how one jurisdiction's rules can become the world's rules through market pressure rather than formal agreement. The clearest example is the European Union, whose regulations often set global standards because multinational companies find it easier to comply with the strictest regime everywhere than to maintain different practices for different markets. The scholar Anu Bradford named this phenomenon the Brussels Effect. When the EU adopted strict data privacy rules under its General Data Protection Regulation, many global companies, including American ones, adjusted their practices worldwide to comply, effectively extending European privacy standards across the globe. The same pattern has appeared with EU rules on chemicals and is emerging with its regulation of artificial intelligence. American companies end up following European rules not because American agencies adopted them, but because the economics of operating globally make the strictest applicable standard the default.

The accountability puzzle. International regulatory cooperation raises questions the domestic framework struggles to answer. The administrative law this book has described is built around domestic processes: notice-and-comment rulemaking, public participation, judicial review, congressional oversight. International standard-setting often happens through negotiations among regulators from many countries, in forums that don't follow the APA and don't provide the participation rights Americans expect for domestic rules. When a standard gets worked out in an international body and then flows into domestic regulation, the public may have had little opportunity to weigh in during the process where the substance was actually decided. This creates a gap in accountability, where consequential regulatory choices get made through channels that bypass the procedures designed to keep agency power legitimate and answerable. As regulation grows more global, the tension between the need for international coordination and the domestic framework's demands for participation and accountability will keep pressing, and the field hasn't yet worked out how to reconcile them.

The Future of Agency Deference Post-Chevron

The single largest change in administrative law in decades was the overruling of Chevron in *Loper Bright Enterprises v. Raimondo* in 2024, covered in the previous chapter. But that decision was less an ending than a beginning. It reset the relationship between agencies and courts, and the consequences are only starting to unfold. Understanding where the field goes from here means looking at the questions *Loper Bright* left open and at the cluster of other recent decisions that, together with it, are remaking the balance of power in the administrative state.

What replaces Chevron. With Chevron gone, courts now interpret the statutes agencies administer independently, without deferring to reasonable agency readings just because a statute is ambiguous. But agency expertise didn't become irrelevant. *Loper Bright* preserved *Skidmore* respect, the older and weaker principle, also discussed earlier, under which courts give an agency's interpretation weight to the extent it's persuasive, considering the thoroughness of the agency's reasoning, the consistency of its position, and its expertise. The trouble is that *Skidmore* is indeterminate. It doesn't tell courts how much weight to give an agency's views; it just says to consider them. This means the actual amount of influence agencies retain over statutory interpretation is now uncertain and will vary from judge to judge and case to case. A judge inclined to respect agency expertise can give an agency's reading substantial weight under *Skidmore*, while a skeptical judge can give it almost none. The predictability Chevron provided, for all its faults, has been replaced by a more open-ended inquiry whose results are harder to forecast.

The stability question. *Loper Bright* tried to limit the disruption its holding would cause. The Court said that prior decisions that had relied on Chevron to uphold specific agency interpretations weren't automatically overruled, and that those holdings retain force under principles of statutory stare decisis. In other words, the fact that a court had previously deferred to an agency's reading under Chevron doesn't mean that reading is now automatically up for grabs. This was meant to prevent a flood of challenges seeking to relitigate every interpretation Chevron had ever blessed. Whether it will actually contain the disruption is unclear. Litigants have strong incentives to test old interpretations under the new, less deferential regime, and lower courts will have to sort out how much protection the prior Chevron-based decisions really retain. The potential for significant churn in settled areas of law is real, and how much of it materializes will shape the field for years.

Corner Post opens the door wider. The disruption potential grew sharply because of a companion decision in the same 2024 term. In *Corner Post, Inc. v. Board of Governors of the Federal Reserve System*, the Court addressed when the clock starts running on the deadline to challenge an agency rule. The general statute of limitations for suing over federal agency action is six years. The question was whether that six years runs from when the rule was issued, or from when a particular plaintiff was injured by it. The Court held that it runs from the plaintiff's injury. This means a business that didn't exist when a rule was adopted, and so couldn't have been injured by it then, can challenge that rule within six years of when the business is first harmed, even if the rule is decades old.

The implications are large. *Corner Post* effectively removes the time bar that would have protected many longstanding rules from challenge, because there will almost always be some newly formed entity that can claim a fresh injury and a fresh six-year window. Combined with the end of Chevron, this creates an opening for challenges to established regulations that were previously insulated by both deference and the passage of time. A newly created company can now attack an old rule, and it can do so under the less deferential standard *Loper Bright* established. Justice Jackson, dissenting, warned that the decision would unleash a wave of litigation against settled rules and destabilize regulatory schemes that businesses and the public had long relied on. Whether the wave arrives as she feared remains to be seen, but the door has clearly been opened wider than it was.

The pieces fit together. These decisions aren't isolated. Taken together, a series of rulings from the 2022 through 2024 Supreme Court terms represents a coordinated reduction in agency power and expansion of judicial control over the administrative state.

Decision	Year	Effect on Agency Power
West Virginia v. EPA	2022	Major questions doctrine limits sweeping agency action
SEC v. Jarkesy	2024	Jury-trial right pulls enforcement out of agency tribunals
Loper Bright v. Raimondo	2024	Courts interpret statutes independently; no Chevron deference

Corner Post v. Federal Reserve	2024	Old rules become vulnerable to fresh challenges

Each of these decisions, discussed at various points in this book, cuts back agency authority from a different angle. The major questions doctrine limits what agencies can do on the biggest issues. *Jarkesy* constrains how agencies can enforce the law, pushing cases into real courts with juries. *Loper Bright* strips agencies of interpretive deference. And *Corner Post* exposes even old rules to challenge. Together they amount to a substantial rebalancing, shifting power away from agencies and toward courts and, in principle, toward Congress. Some describe this as a reining-in of an administrative state that had grown too powerful; others describe it as a judicial power grab that will hamstring the government's ability to address complex problems. Both descriptions capture something real about the magnitude of the change.

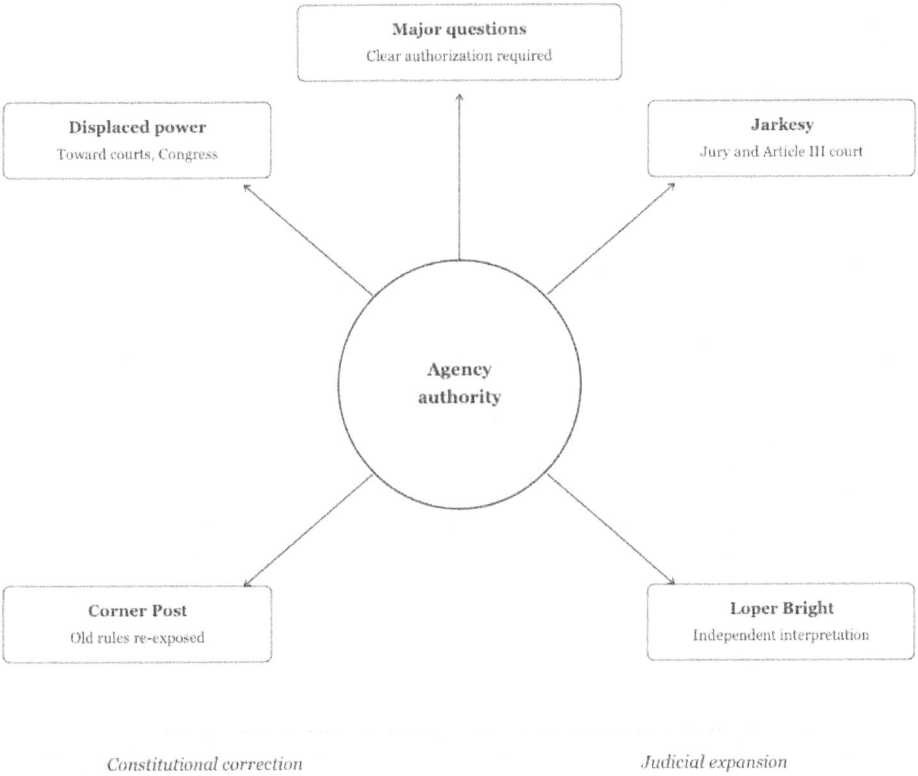

Nondelegation waiting in the wings. There's reason to think the rebalancing may not be finished. The nondelegation doctrine, discussed in the first chapter of this book, has been nearly dormant since 1935, but several justices signaled in *Gundy v. United States* in 2019 that they'd be willing to revive it and demand that Congress provide more specific guidance before delegating power to agencies. If the Court did revive nondelegation, it would add yet another constraint on top of the major questions doctrine and the end of Chevron. Agencies would face a constitutional limit on how much power Congress could give them in the first place, a statutory-interpretation hurdle for their biggest actions, and independent judicial review of their ordinary interpretations. The combination would represent the most substantial constraint on administrative power since the modern regulatory state took shape. Whether the Court takes this further step is one of the open questions hanging over the field's future.

Congress in the middle. All of this puts new pressure on Congress. As courts grow less willing to let agencies fill statutory gaps and stretch old statutes to new problems, the responsibility for making policy shifts back toward the legislature that's supposed to make it. In theory, this is a return to constitutional first principles: Congress makes the laws, and agencies carry them out within clear boundaries. In practice, Congress is often gridlocked, struggling to pass major legislation and reluctant to write the detailed statutes that the new judicial approach seems to require.

This creates a potential gap. If courts won't let agencies act without clear authorization, and Congress can't or won't provide that authorization, the result may be that certain problems go unaddressed, with neither agencies nor Congress able to act. The alternative is that more policymaking flows through litigation, as courts decide what statutes mean and thereby shape policy through their interpretations. Either way, the practical effect of reining in agencies depends heavily on whether Congress rises to the role the new regime assigns it, and that remains very much in doubt.

The future of administrative law, then, is a future of renegotiation. The balance among Congress, agencies, and courts that held for much of the past century is being redrawn, and the direction is clear even if the destination isn't. Courts are reclaiming authority they'd ceded to agencies. Agencies face more constraints and more skepticism than they have in generations. And Congress finds itself pushed toward a more active role it may not be equipped to fill. Add to this the new challenges of artificial intelligence, the pull of global regulation, and the experiments unfolding in the states, and the picture is of a field in genuine flux, working out fundamental questions about how a modern government should exercise power that the framers of the Administrative Procedure Act thought they'd settled. Those questions are open again, and how they're answered will shape American government for a long time to come.

Discussion Question

The Supreme Court's recent decisions all share a premise: that agencies had accumulated too much power, and that returning authority to courts and Congress restores the constitutional design. But this assumes Congress can actually do the job being handed back to it, writing detailed statutes and updating them as problems evolve, at a moment when Congress can barely pass a budget. If reining in agencies simply means that hard problems go unsolved because neither agencies nor a gridlocked Congress can act, has the country really restored the separation of powers, or has it just made the government less capable of governing? And if you had to choose, would you rather have powerful agencies that sometimes overreach, or constrained agencies that sometimes can't act at all?

Historical Timeline of Administrative Law

The story below traces administrative law from a government with almost no agencies to the sprawling regulatory system of today, and through the long argument over who gets to control it.

1789, the first executive departments. In its opening year under the Constitution, Congress built the skeleton of the executive branch by creating three departments: State to handle foreign affairs, Treasury to manage the nation's money, and War, the ancestor of today's Department of Defense. These weren't regulatory agencies in the modern sense. They administered the basic functions of a small national government. But they established the pattern of Congress creating bodies by statute, defining their duties, and staffing them with officials the president appointed, which is the seed everything else grew from.

1789, the Judiciary Act. The same Congress passed the Judiciary Act, organizing the federal court system that would one day review agency action, though no such action yet existed to review.

1803, Marbury v. Madison. Chief Justice John Marshall's opinion established that courts have the power to review government action and strike down what violates the law, declaring that it's the job of the judiciary to say what the law is. That principle sat mostly dormant with respect to agencies for over a century, but it's the foundation on which all judicial review of agency action eventually rested.

1825, Wayman v. Southard. Marshall confronted an early version of the delegation question, whether Congress could let the courts make rules of procedure. He acknowledged that Congress may delegate authority to fill in details on subjects it can't manage itself, drawing a rough line between important matters Congress must decide and lesser ones it can hand off. The idea would echo through the nondelegation debates a century later.

1870, the Department of Justice. Congress consolidated the government's legal work under a new department headed by the attorney general, gathering the federal lawyers into one house.

1887, the Interstate Commerce Commission. This is the birth of the modern regulatory state, and it came from the railroads. By the 1880s, railroads dominated the American economy and abused that dominance, charging farmers punishing rates, granting secret rebates to favored shippers, and wielding monopoly power in ways that infuriated the public. State laws couldn't reach a business that crossed state lines, and Congress had no way to write detailed, constantly changing rate rules on its own. So Congress tried something new. It created a permanent commission of experts, gave it a mission, and let it regulate railroad rates on an ongoing basis. The

Interstate Commerce Commission could investigate, hold hearings, and issue orders, combining functions the Constitution had seemed to separate into one body. The experiment struggled at first, because early court decisions gutted much of the commission's authority, and it took later statutes to give it real power. But the model itself proved durable, and it became the template for nearly every agency that followed. The insight behind it, that some subjects are too technical and too fast-moving for a part-time legislature of generalists to manage directly, and that a body of specialists working full-time can do what Congress can't, is the justification for the entire administrative state. Everything in this timeline after 1887 builds on the choice made that year.

1906, food, drugs, and railroad teeth. Public alarm over filthy meatpacking plants and dangerous patent medicines, brought to light by Upton Sinclair's *The Jungle*, amplified by muckraking journalism, pushed through the Pure Food and Drug Act and the Meat Inspection Act in a single year, giving the federal government new authority over what Americans ate and swallowed. The same year, the Hepburn Act finally gave the Interstate Commerce Commission the power to set maximum railroad rates, curing much of the weakness that had hobbled it since 1887. Together these laws marked the government's move into protecting consumers and controlling industry, the beginning of the Progressive Era's regulatory expansion.

1908, Londoner v. Denver. The Supreme Court held that when a city imposed a special tax on a small group of specific property owners, those individuals were entitled to a hearing first, because the action turned on facts particular to them. The case drew an early line between individualized decisions that require a hearing and general ones that don't.

1913, the Federal Reserve and the Department of Labor. Congress created the Federal Reserve to manage the nation's money and banking, building an institution with unusual insulation from political control that would become the model of an independent agency. The same year saw the Department of Labor established, giving workers a cabinet-level voice. Both reflected a government taking on responsibilities it had left alone before, and the Fed in particular showed Congress deliberately designing an agency to resist the political pressures of the moment.

1914, the Federal Trade Commission. Congress created the FTC to police unfair methods of competition and unfair business practices, adding another independent commission to the growing structure and giving the government a general watchdog over corporate behavior.

1915, Bi-Metallic v. State Board of Equalization. Justice Holmes wrote that when Colorado raised property valuations across an entire city, affecting everyone who owned property there, no individual hearings were required. When government action applies generally to a large group, he reasoned, people's remedy is political, through the ballot, not through personal hearings. Paired with Londoner, this case fixed the basic distinction that still separates rulemaking from adjudication.

1926, Myers v. United States. Chief Justice William Howard Taft, who'd been president himself, wrote a sweeping opinion striking down a law that required Senate consent before the president could remove certain postmasters. The president, he held, has broad constitutional power to remove executive officers, because the president must be able to control the people who carry out the laws. Myers seemed to establish a strong presidential removal power, though the Court would carve out a major exception within a decade.

1928, J.W. Hampton v. United States. The Court settled on the compromise that let the administrative state function. Congress can delegate authority to an agency, it held, as long as it lays down an "intelligible principle" to guide the agency's decisions. Congress doesn't have to write every detail; it just has to give a clear enough standard that the agency is filling in blanks rather than writing law from scratch. This test became the near-permanent answer to the nondelegation problem, and its leniency is why almost no delegation has failed since.

1933, the New Deal begins. Franklin Roosevelt took office amid the Great Depression, and the flood of new agencies started immediately. The Securities Act of 1933 required companies selling securities to the public to register them and disclose the truth about their finances, the first piece of the disclosure-based system that would define federal securities regulation. It was the opening move in a transformation that would build most of the modern regulatory state in just a few years.

1934, the SEC and the FCC. Congress created the Securities and Exchange Commission to police the stock markets after the 1929 crash wiped out millions of investors, and it passed the Securities Exchange Act governing the ongoing life of public companies. The same year brought the Federal Communications Commission and the Communications Act, putting broadcasting and telephones under federal control. Two more independent commissions joined the structure, each taking charge of a slice of the economy that had grown too important to leave unregulated.

1935, the pivotal year. No single year did more to shape administrative law, and it pulled in opposite directions at once. The Supreme Court struck down federal laws for excessive delegation, the only two times it has ever done so. In Panama Refining Co. v. Ryan, the "hot oil" case, it found that Congress had given the president power to ban interstate oil shipments with almost no guidance. A few months later, in A.L.A. Schechter Poultry Corp. v. United States, the "sick chicken" case, it killed a core piece of New Deal legislation that let industry groups and the president write "codes of fair competition" with barely any standards at all. These two decisions are the entire history of successful nondelegation challenges at the Court. Yet the same year, in Humphrey's Executor v. United States, the Court moved the other way on presidential power, holding that Congress could protect the leaders of independent commissions like the FTC from being fired at will, because those agencies did quasi-legislative and quasi-judicial work, not purely executive tasks. Humphrey's Executor became the constitutional foundation for every independent agency. And beyond the courtroom, Congress passed the National Labor Relations Act, creating the National Labor Relations Board to referee union organizing, and the Social Security Act, building the retirement and benefits system that would generate one of the largest adjudication operations in the world. In twelve months, the Court both checked and blessed the administrative state while Congress kept expanding it.

1938, food and wages. The Federal Food, Drug, and Cosmetic Act rebuilt the FDA's authority over drugs and food, and the Fair Labor Standards Act established the minimum wage, overtime pay, and limits on child labor, adding another pillar to the growing body of federal regulation over daily economic life.

1940, the Walter-Logan veto. Congress passed the Walter-Logan Act, an early attempt to impose uniform procedures on agencies, but Roosevelt vetoed it, seeing it as an effort to hobble the agencies he'd built. The veto delayed procedural reform but signaled how badly the system needed a common set of rules that both sides could accept.

1941, the Attorney General's report. A committee assembled by the attorney general produced a detailed study of administrative procedure, documenting how inconsistently agencies operated and laying the intellectual groundwork for the reform that would come after the war.

1944, Skidmore v. Swift. The Court described a modest form of deference, holding that an agency's interpretation deserves weight based on its persuasiveness, considering the thoroughness of its reasoning and the consistency of its position. Skidmore isn't binding deference; it's respect. The court makes its own call but takes the agency's views seriously when they're well-reasoned. Overshadowed for decades, this standard would return to prominence when Chevron fell.

1945, Seminole Rock. In Bowles v. Seminole Rock, the Court held that an agency's interpretation of its own regulation controls unless plainly wrong, planting the seed of what later became Auer deference.

1946, the Administrative Procedure Act. After years of study and negotiation, Congress passed the master statute of federal administrative law, and President Truman signed it. The APA brought order to a system that had grown chaotic, with every agency following its own procedures and no consistent rules for how to write a regulation or run a hearing. The Act sorted nearly everything agencies do into two categories, rulemaking and adjudication, and set procedures for each, distinguishing formal trial-type proceedings from informal ones. Its Section 553 established notice-and-comment rulemaking, the process by which most federal regulations are still made. Its Section 706 told courts how to review agency action, including the "arbitrary and capricious" standard that became one of the most litigated phrases in the field. The statute passed without serious opposition, reflecting how much both the agencies' defenders and their critics wanted a common framework. People sometimes call it the constitution of administrative law, and the description fits, because almost everything in the field runs through it. Yet the APA is remarkably brief and skeletal, leaving many of the details that matter most unstated, which meant courts would spend the next seventy-plus years filling in the blanks with a vast body of case law. The same year, in Oklahoma Press Publishing Co. v. Walling, the Court upheld broad agency subpoena power, setting the forgiving standard for when agencies can compel information.

1947, Chenery II. In SEC v. Chenery Corp., the Court held that agencies may make policy through case-by-case adjudication rather than through rulemaking, giving them a choice of methods. The NLRB would embrace this approach more fully than any other agency, building its entire body of labor doctrine through decisions.

1950, United States v. Morton Salt. The Court held that an agency doesn't need probable cause or even specific suspicion to investigate. It can act on what the Court called a kind of official curiosity, investigating simply to satisfy itself that regulated parties are following the law. This confirmed how much lower the bar is for an administrative subpoena than for a criminal search.

1952, Youngstown Sheet & Tube v. Sawyer. When President Truman seized the nation's steel mills to prevent a strike from crippling production during the Korean War, the Court ruled against him, finding he had no statutory or constitutional authority to take private property this way. The lasting contribution wasn't the majority opinion but Justice Robert Jackson's concurrence, which laid out a three-part framework for judging presidential power that courts still use. Presidential authority is highest when the president acts with congressional authorization, uncertain when Congress is silent, and at its lowest ebb when the president acts against Congress's will. Truman's seizure fell into that weakest category, because Congress had considered giving presidents seizure power and declined. Jackson turned a single wartime dispute into the enduring tool for measuring the limits of executive authority, including the limits on executive orders directing agencies.

1966, the Freedom of Information Act. Congress gave any person the right to request records from federal agencies, resting the whole statute on a simple principle: the government's records belong to the public. FOIA established a default rule that agencies must disclose records when asked, putting the burden on the government to justify withholding rather than on the requester to justify access. A requester doesn't even have to give a reason. The statute contained nine exemptions covering things like national security, trade secrets, and internal deliberations, and those exemptions would become the heart of decades of litigation. FOIA became the primary way journalists, researchers, and ordinary citizens could find out what their government was actually doing. The same year, Congress created the Department of Transportation.

1967, Abbott Laboratories v. Gardner. The Court set out the ripeness test for challenges to agency rules, weighing the fitness of the issues for judicial decision against the hardship to the parties of withholding review. A purely legal challenge to a rule with immediate impact could go forward even before enforcement, the Court held, opening the courthouse door to pre-enforcement challenges.

1970, the second great wave. A single year produced much of the modern regulatory government, and much of it happened under a Republican president. Richard Nixon's administration created the Environmental Protection Agency by executive reorganization, pulling scattered environmental responsibilities into one agency, and Congress passed a strengthened Clean Air Act directing the EPA to set national air quality standards. Congress also passed the Occupational Safety and Health Act, creating OSHA to regulate workplace safety, and established the National Highway Traffic Safety Administration to make cars safer. The public's concern had shifted toward the environment, consumer safety, and worker health, and the government responded by building agencies whose rules still shape the air people breathe, the cars they drive, and the conditions they work in. The same year, in Goldberg v. Kelly, the Supreme Court held that welfare benefits are a form of property protected by due process, and that the government couldn't cut them off without first giving the recipient an evidentiary hearing. For someone dependent on those benefits, a mistaken termination could be devastating, and the Court found the stakes demanded a hearing before the cutoff, not after. Goldberg established that government benefits aren't a mere privilege the state can withdraw at will.

1971, Citizens to Preserve Overton Park v. Volpe. The Court described what arbitrary and capricious review actually requires, directing courts to examine the full administrative record and ask whether the agency considered the relevant factors and made a clear error of judgment. The decision made clear that judicial review of agency discretion would have real substance, not just rubber-stamp deference.

1972, the Clean Water Act. Congress overhauled federal control of water pollution, building the permit system that regulates what facilities can discharge into the nation's waters. The same year brought the Consumer Product Safety Commission, adding another agency to protect the public from dangerous products.

1973, Florida East Coast Railway and Vaughn v. Rosen. In United States v. Florida East Coast Railway, the Court held that formal rulemaking, the trial-type process, is required only when a statute clearly demands a decision "on the record after a hearing." Because Congress rarely uses those exact words, formal rulemaking nearly vanished. The same year, in Vaughn v. Rosen, a court created the index that lets FOIA litigation function, requiring agencies to describe each withheld document and explain why an exemption applies, so courts and requesters can evaluate the claims without examining every secret document.

1976, Mathews v. Eldridge and the Sunshine Act. The Court gave due process its enduring test in Mathews v. Eldridge, a case about terminating Social Security disability benefits. It laid out three factors to weigh in deciding how much process any situation demands: the importance of the private interest at stake, the risk of an erroneous decision and whether more procedure would reduce it, and the burden additional procedures would impose on the government. Balancing these, the Court held that a hearing after termination, rather than before, was enough for disability benefits. The test made clear that due process is flexible, demanding more when stakes are high and less when they're not. The same year, the Government in the Sunshine Act required multimember agencies to hold their meetings in public, and Congress passed major statutes on hazardous waste and toxic chemicals, expanding the EPA's reach.

1978, Vermont Yankee, Barlow's, and the Inspector General Act. In Vermont Yankee Nuclear Power Corp. v. NRDC, the Court firmly shut down the practice of lower courts imposing extra procedural requirements on agencies beyond what the APA demanded. If the statute says notice and comment is enough, then it's enough, and judges can't require more. The same year, in Marshall v. Barlow's, Inc., the Court held that OSHA generally needs a warrant to inspect a business over the owner's objection, though the warrant standard for an administrative inspection is lower than for a criminal search. And Congress passed the Inspector General Act, creating independent watchdogs inside agencies across the government, each empowered to audit programs and investigate misconduct while reporting both to the agency head and directly to Congress, so the agency couldn't bury what they found.

1979, Chrysler v. Brown. The Court established how reverse-FOIA suits proceed, the cases where a business sues to stop an agency from releasing information it had submitted. The same year, Congress created the Department of Education.

1980, CERCLA and paperwork control. Congress passed the Comprehensive Environmental Response, Compensation, and Liability Act, known as Superfund, creating a system to clean up contaminated sites and impose liability for the contamination. Congress also passed the Paperwork Reduction Act, an early attempt to control the burden agencies impose through their information demands.

1983, State Farm and Chadha. In Motor Vehicle Manufacturers Association v. State Farm, the Court struck down an agency's rescission of a rule requiring airbags or automatic seatbelts, and in doing so it spelled out the modern arbitrary and capricious standard. An agency acts arbitrarily if it ignores an important aspect of the problem, offers an explanation contrary to the evidence, or fails to consider an obvious alternative, as the agency had done by scrapping the whole rule instead of considering an airbag-only requirement. State Farm established "hard look" review, under which courts check that the agency genuinely engaged with the evidence and alternatives. The same year, in INS v. Chadha, the Court struck down the legislative veto, the device by which Congress had reserved the power to overturn agency actions by resolution without going through the full lawmaking process. The decision invalidated provisions in dozens of statutes and reshaped how Congress could control agencies.

1984, Chevron v. NRDC. No decision shaped modern administrative law more, though no one recognized it as a landmark at the time. The case involved the EPA's interpretation of a technical term in the Clean Air Act, and in resolving it the Court announced a two-step framework for reviewing an agency's reading of a statute it administers. At step one, if Congress has clearly spoken to the question, that clear meaning controls. At step two, if the statute is silent or ambiguous, the court doesn't impose its own reading; it asks only whether the agency's interpretation is reasonable, and if it is, the court defers, even if it would have chosen differently. The theory was that statutory ambiguity signals an implicit delegation to the expert, politically accountable agency to fill the gap. For forty years, Chevron made agencies powerful, because whenever a statute was less than perfectly clear, and statutes often are, the agency's interpretation usually prevailed. It became the single most cited decision in the field and defined the balance of power between agencies and courts for a generation, until the Court overruled it in 2024.

1985, Heckler v. Chaney. The Court held that an agency's decision not to take enforcement action is presumptively unreviewable, reasoning that enforcement choices involve balancing priorities and resources in ways courts aren't well suited to second-guess. This gave agencies significant room to soften regulation through non-enforcement, though the presumption isn't absolute and doesn't let an agency abandon a mandatory statutory duty.

1987, Tull and Burger. In Tull v. United States, the Court held that when the government sues for civil penalties in court, the defendant is entitled to a jury trial, because such an action is the kind the Seventh Amendment covers. In New York v. Burger, it upheld a warrantless inspection of a vehicle dismantling business, applying the exception for closely regulated industries where operators have a reduced expectation of privacy.

1988, Morrison v. Olson. The Court upheld a law protecting an independent counsel from at-will removal, applying a functional test and asking whether the protection stopped the president from carrying out his constitutional duties. It concluded the protection didn't, and the vote was seven to one. The lone dissenter was Justice Antonin Scalia, who argued that the president must have complete control over anyone exercising executive power. At the time his view lost, but over the following decades it gained ground, and his dissent is now cited more often than the majority he was writing against.

1989, the Whistleblower Protection Act. Congress strengthened protections for federal employees who report wrongdoing, prohibiting agencies from retaliating against those who make protected disclosures and creating a system to enforce the prohibition. The same year, Congress elevated veterans' affairs to a cabinet department.

1992, Lujan v. Defenders of Wildlife. Justice Scalia laid out the three-part test for standing that every plaintiff challenging agency action must satisfy: a concrete and imminent injury in fact, causation traceable to the challenged action, and redressability by a favorable decision. The Court found that environmental groups claiming they might someday travel abroad to see endangered species hadn't shown imminent injury. Caring about an issue, the decision made clear, isn't the same as being harmed by it, and standing would remain a real barrier keeping many objections out of court.

1993, Executive Order 12866. President Clinton established the system of centralized review that still governs major rulemaking, requiring agencies to analyze the costs and benefits of significant rules and submit them to an office inside the White House for review before they take effect. Building on an earlier Reagan order, it gave the president a check on what agencies produce, and it has survived across administrations of both parties.

1994, MCI v. AT&T. The Court held that the FCC couldn't use its authority to "modify" rate-filing requirements to eliminate them for most carriers, because a change that sweeping couldn't hide in a word as modest as "modify." The decision planted an early seed of what would become the major questions doctrine.

1996, the Congressional Review Act. Congress gave itself a streamlined tool to overturn agency rules, requiring agencies to submit final rules for review and letting Congress pass a joint resolution of disapproval within a set window. The tool's power came from a procedural feature: in the Senate, a disapproval resolution can't be filibustered, so it needs only a simple majority. For two decades the CRA sat almost entirely unused, successful just once, but it would suddenly become a real force after a change in party control aligned Congress and the presidency.

2000, FDA v. Brown & Williamson. The Court held that the FDA had overstepped its statutory authority when it tried to regulate tobacco, reasoning that Congress had repeatedly addressed tobacco through separate, specific laws while keeping it out of the agency's hands. The decision wasn't about whether regulating tobacco was wise; it was about whether the agency's enabling statute stretched that far, and the Court concluded it didn't. Congress supplied the missing authority nine years later.

2001, Whitman and Mead. In Whitman v. American Trucking Associations, the Court upheld the Clean Air Act's instruction to set air standards "requisite to protect the public health" against a nondelegation challenge, with Justice Scalia making clear the Court had almost never found a delegation too broad. In United States v. Mead Corp., the Court limited when Chevron deference applies, holding that it governs only when Congress gave the agency authority to make rules with the force of law and the agency acted under that authority; less formal agency documents would get only the weaker Skidmore respect. The same year, Congress used the CRA for the first time, repealing an OSHA ergonomics rule.

2002, the Department of Homeland Security. In response to the September 11 attacks, Congress pulled dozens of existing agencies into a single new department focused on security, the largest reorganization of the federal government in half a century.

2007, Massachusetts v. EPA. The Court held that greenhouse gases are air pollutants under the Clean Air Act and that the EPA couldn't simply refuse to decide whether they endanger public health. The ruling didn't force any particular rule; it stripped away the agency's claim that it could walk away from the question entirely, converting a subject the agency preferred to avoid into a duty it had to confront. The Court also gave states "special solicitude" in the standing analysis, letting Massachusetts sue over the loss of coastal land to rising seas.

2009, FCC v. Fox and tobacco authority. In FCC v. Fox Television Stations, the Court held that an agency reversing a prior policy doesn't have to prove the new policy is better, but it does have to acknowledge that it's changing course and give reasons. The same year, Congress passed the Family Smoking Prevention and Tobacco Control Act, finally giving the FDA explicit authority over tobacco and reversing the result of Brown & Williamson.

2010, Free Enterprise Fund and Dodd-Frank. In Free Enterprise Fund v. Public Company Accounting Oversight Board, the Court struck down "double for-cause" removal protection, holding that stacking two layers of insulation stripped the president of the control the Constitution requires. The same year, responding to the 2008 financial crisis, Congress passed the Dodd-Frank Act, a sweeping overhaul that created the Consumer Financial Protection Bureau, expanded regulation of derivatives and large financial institutions, and directed agencies to write dozens of new rules, generating years of rulemaking.

2015, King v. Burwell and Michigan v. EPA. In King v. Burwell, the Court declined to apply Chevron to a question of deep economic and political importance under the Affordable Care Act, deciding the statutory question itself and planting the seed of the major questions doctrine. In Michigan v. EPA, it held that the agency had unreasonably failed to consider costs when deciding whether to regulate power plant emissions, applying arbitrary and capricious principles to the question of when cost has to enter the analysis.

2018, Lucia and the states move first. In Lucia v. SEC, the Court held that the agency's administrative law judges are officers of the United States who must be appointed under the Appointments Clause, not simply hired, forcing agencies to change how they installed their judges. The same year, states raced ahead of the federal courts on deference. The Wisconsin Supreme Court ended deference to state agency interpretations, Arizona enacted a statute directing courts to decide legal questions independently, and Florida amended its constitution to prohibit state courts from deferring to agencies at all. The states ran the experiment that the federal courts wouldn't reach until 2024.

2019, Gundy, Kisor, and pretext. In Gundy v. United States, the Court upheld a delegation but only barely, with four justices signaling real interest in reviving a stronger nondelegation doctrine and Justice Gorsuch arguing at length that the intelligible principle test had strayed too far from the Constitution. In Kisor v. Wilkie, the Court declined to overrule Auer deference to an agency's reading of its own regulations but narrowed it sharply, limiting it to genuinely ambiguous rules. And in Department of Commerce v. New York, the Court blocked the addition of a citizenship question to the census, finding the agency's stated rationale appeared to be pretextual, and holding that courts aren't required to accept a contrived explanation.

2020, Seila Law and the pandemic. In Seila Law v. Consumer Financial Protection Bureau, the Court struck down the removal protection for the CFPB's single director, holding that concentrating so much power in one official insulated from presidential control violated the separation of powers. It kept the agency alive by making the director removable at will. The same year, as COVID-19 spread, agencies across the government issued interim final rules under the good cause exemption, waiving normal procedures to respond to the emergency, in what became a large-scale test of when agencies can skip notice and comment.

2022, West Virginia v. EPA and the vaccine mandate. The Court formally named the major questions doctrine in West Virginia v. EPA, striking down the agency's attempt to force a broad shift in how the nation generates electricity and holding that a transformation of that magnitude required clear congressional authorization the statute didn't provide. Months earlier, in NFIB v. OSHA, the Court had blocked OSHA's rule requiring large employers to mandate vaccination or testing, reasoning that a public health measure affecting tens of millions of workers exceeded the agency's clear authority. Together these decisions showed the doctrine's force even in an emergency.

2024, the year of realignment. The Supreme Court delivered a cluster of decisions that rebalanced the entire administrative state. In SEC v. Jarkesy, it held that when the government pursues civil penalties for fraud, the Seventh Amendment entitles the defendant to a jury trial in a real court, not a hearing before the agency's own judge, calling into question the in-house adjudication many agencies rely on. In Loper Bright Enterprises v. Raimondo, the herring fishermen's case, it overruled Chevron after forty years, holding that courts must exercise their own independent judgment in interpreting the statutes agencies administer and may not defer to an agency's reading just because a statute is ambiguous. The Court grounded the decision in the APA's command that courts decide questions of law, and it preserved only the weaker Skidmore respect for agency views. And in Corner Post v. Board of Governors of the Federal Reserve System, it held that the six-year clock for challenging a rule runs from when a plaintiff is injured, not from when the rule was issued, meaning a newly formed business can attack even a decades-old regulation. Taken together with the major questions doctrine and the stirring of nondelegation, these decisions shifted power away from agencies and toward courts and Congress, reopening fundamental questions about how a modern government should exercise power that the drafters of the Administrative Procedure Act once thought they'd settled.

End-of-Chapter Discussion Questions

Chapter 1. When an unelected expert makes a decision as consequential as Kelsey's, where's the line between trusting expertise and demanding accountability, and does it matter whether the expert turns out right?

The Kelsey story tempts us to say expertise should win, but that's partly hindsight talking. She turned out right, and being right makes the case for expert judgment look obvious. The harder test is the expert who turns out wrong, like the Michigan fraud algorithm that falsely accused tens of thousands of people. Accountability matters precisely because we can't know in advance who's Kelsey and who's mistaken. The workable answer isn't choosing between expertise and accountability; it's building accountability around expertise. Kelsey answered to no voter, but she operated under a statute Congress wrote, her decisions could be reviewed, and Congress could change the law if it disagreed, which it did through the 1962 amendments that strengthened drug approval. That layered structure lets experts exercise judgment while keeping the system answerable. So the line shouldn't shift based on outcomes. A structure that only demands accountability when the expert gets it wrong isn't accountability at all. It's just second-guessing after the fact, and it would punish the careful Kelseys along with the reckless ones.

Chapter 2. If every agency head became removable at will by the president, what would the country gain and lose, and are there functions that shouldn't bend to electoral politics?

The gain is accountability and coherence. A president elected on a platform could actually direct the whole executive branch, and voters would have a clearer target to hold responsible. The loss is stability in areas where swinging with each election does real damage. The Federal Reserve is the strongest case. If interest rates moved to serve whoever's up for reelection, markets would lose the confidence that comes from believing monetary policy tracks the economy rather than the campaign calendar. Some functions, like setting rates, running fair elections, and deciding whether to prosecute a specific person, work better with distance from politics. Not because democracy is bad, but because the temptation to abuse those particular powers for political advantage is too strong to leave unchecked.

Chapter 3. When does interpreting a vague grant count as carrying out Congress's delegation, and when is it the agency seizing power Congress never gave? Is there a workable test, or does it come down to whether a judge likes the result?

The honest answer is that there's no clean test, and everyone who works in this field knows it. The tobacco case shows why. The FDA read "drug" and "device" to cover cigarettes, which deliver nicotine, a drug. That reading wasn't unreasonable on the words alone. The Court rejected it anyway, looking past the text to what Congress had actually done about tobacco over the decades. Whether you call that faithful interpretation or judicial preference depends partly on where you started.

Still, some signals help separate the two, even if they don't decide every case. When an agency suddenly discovers vast power in an old statute nobody had read that way, skepticism is warranted, which is the instinct behind the major questions doctrine. When an agency's reading fits the statute's structure and history and matches how the law has long operated, it looks more like execution than seizure. When the reading would force the agency into something absurd, like banning the very product it claims authority over, something has clearly gone wrong.

The uncomfortable truth is that these signals guide judgment without eliminating it, so the philosophy of the judge will always matter. Nobody has figured out how to fix that. It's the reason the end of Chevron shifted so much power simply by changing who resolves the ambiguity.

Chapter 4. Did courts, by making rulemaking more thorough, weaken the public's voice instead of strengthening it? Would a faster process agencies actually used be a better deal?

Probably yes on the first question. Each requirement courts added made notice-and-comment slower and costlier, and the predictable result is that agencies now dodge it, using guidance documents that bind in practice while skipping the comment period. A protection so heavy that people route around it protects no one. A lighter process agencies actually used might give the public more real influence than an elaborate one they avoid. The catch is that "lighter" can slide into "no participation at all," so the trick is trimming the burden without gutting the input itself.

Chapter 5. If Jarkesy forces enforcement into slow, costly courts and agencies bring fewer cases, have we traded one unfairness for another? Where's the balance between full court protection and the ability to enforce at all?

There's a real trade here, and pretending otherwise doesn't help. The agency courtroom was efficient, and that efficiency let agencies bring cases they couldn't afford to bring in federal court. Jarkesy protects the accused party's right to a jury, which matters most exactly when the government comes after someone for something like fraud. But if the practical effect is that the SEC brings a third fewer cases because each one now costs far more, then a lot of wrongdoing goes unpunished, and the people harmed by that fraud lose something too.

Where to strike it probably depends on what's at stake for the accused. The heavier the penalty and the more it resembles a traditional legal wrong, the stronger the case for a real court with a jury. Minor, technical, regulatory fines in specialized fields make a weaker case for full trial machinery. A sensible system might reserve the jury guarantee for the serious, fraud-like penalties Jarkesy worried about while leaving routine administrative fines in the faster process. The mistake would be treating this as all-or-nothing, because both the accused party's protection and the public's interest in enforcement are real, and neither should be sacrificed completely to the other.

Chapter 6. Which produces more honest government, Chevron deference or Loper Bright's independent review? Does the answer depend on whether you trust agencies or courts more?

Yes, the answer largely tracks who you trust more, which is why reasonable people land in different places. If you think agencies are expert bodies doing their best to carry out congressional will, Chevron looks right, because it lets the people who know the subject resolve the gaps. If you think agencies stretch ambiguous statutes to grab power and shift their readings with each administration, independent judicial review looks right, because it puts a neutral party in charge of what the law means. Both can claim the rule of law. Chevron's version values consistency through expertise and keeps policy with a politically accountable branch. Loper Bright's version values a fixed meaning that doesn't lurch when the White House changes hands. The real question underneath is whether statutory meaning should be stable or responsive, and that's a genuine disagreement, not a puzzle with one correct answer.

Chapter 7. How much of accountability rests on legal structures versus the character of the people involved? If the structures stay but the will to use them fades, do the paper protections mean anything?

The structures are necessary but not sufficient. FOIA gives you the right to records, but someone has to file the request and litigate when the agency stalls. An inspector general has independence, but someone has to be willing to expose their own agency. The laws create the openings; people decide whether to walk through them. Paper protections that nobody uses mean very little, which is why the Phoenix VA scandal needed a doctor willing to talk before any of the machinery moved.

Chapter 8. Is one regulatory model clearly better, or does it depend on the problem? What does it say that these three systems never became a coherent whole?

No model wins across the board, and the reason is that each fits its problem. Hard standards make sense for pollution, where the harm is physical, science can set a number, and you want a floor nobody drops below. Disclosure makes sense for securities, where the government can't sensibly judge whether every investment is wise but can insist companies tell the truth and let millions of investors decide. Case-by-case adjudication fits labor, where disputes turn on specific facts and the relationships are ongoing. Forcing any one approach onto all three would produce worse results. Picture the SEC deciding which stocks are good enough to sell, or the EPA policing pollution one lawsuit at a time.

That these systems never got knit together says something honest about how American government grew. It wasn't built from a blueprint. Congress added protections one crisis at a time: the securities laws after the 1929 crash, the labor board during the New Deal, the environmental agencies in the 1970s, each shaped by the tools and assumptions of its moment. The result is a patchwork, which frustrates anyone who wants tidy structure. But the patchwork also carries a practical strength, because each piece was built for the specific problem it faced rather than forced to fit a theory imposed from above. Coherence would have looked neater and might well have fit worse.

Chapter 9. If reining in agencies means hard problems go unsolved because neither agencies nor a gridlocked Congress can act, have we restored the separation of powers or just made government less capable? Powerful agencies that overreach, or constrained ones that can't act?

Restoring the separation of powers only works if Congress actually picks up the job being handed back. The Court's recent decisions assume a Congress that writes detailed statutes and updates them as problems change. The Congress we have struggles to pass a budget. So there's a real risk that reining in agencies doesn't relocate power to the legislature; it just leaves problems unaddressed while everyone waits for a Congress that won't move. Forced to choose, I'd weigh how reversible each failure is. An agency that overreaches can be checked by courts, by voters, and by the next administration. A problem left to fester because nobody can act may do lasting damage before the system catches up. Neither option is good, which is rather the point of the question.

Conclusion

You started this book with a number: more than 180,000 pages of federal rules, almost none of them written by anyone you voted for. By now that fact should feel less strange, because you understand the machinery that produces those pages and the long argument over who gets to control it.

The core idea is simple once you see it. Congress can't run a modern country by itself. It can't set the safe level of every pollutant, review every new drug, or referee every labor dispute. So it creates agencies, hands them broad goals, and lets experts fill in the details. That single move, first made with the railroads in 1887, built the government we live under. Everything else in this book follows from it: the rules about how agencies get their power, how they use it, and how they get checked.

That checking is where the real drama lives. Agencies combine powers the Constitution tried to keep separate, writing rules like a legislature, enforcing them like an executive, and deciding cases like a court. That combination has never sat comfortably with the founding design, and the tension has produced a century of fights over how much power agencies should hold. Courts push back through judicial review. Congress pushes back through oversight, funding, and the occasional cancelled rule. Presidents push and pull through appointments and orders. The public pushes through comments, records requests, and lawsuits. None of these checks works perfectly, but together they keep agencies answerable.

What makes this a genuinely interesting moment to study the field is that the balance is shifting under our feet. For forty years, courts mostly deferred to agencies on questions of law. In 2024, they stopped. The major questions doctrine now blocks agencies from their most ambitious moves. Jarkesy is pulling enforcement out of agency courtrooms and into real ones. Corner Post has exposed even old rules to fresh challenges. Taken together, these decisions are moving power away from agencies and toward courts and, in theory, toward Congress. Whether Congress can actually carry that weight is one of the open questions this book leaves you with.

You now have the tools to follow all of it. When you read that a court struck down a rule, you can ask whether the problem was the agency's authority, its procedure, or its reasoning. When an agency claims a new power, you can ask where in its statute that power lives. When you see a news story about a regulation, you can tell what stage it's in and what comes next. These are practical skills, useful whether you work in law, business, or policy, or just want to understand how your government actually operates behind the headlines.

The rules that govern your food, your air, your money, and your job all run through this system. It's imperfect, contested, and always changing. In the end, the measure of administrative government is not how many rules it can write, but whether it can exercise necessary power without forgetting whom that power belongs to.

Key Terms and Definitions

- **Administrative law** - The body of rules governing what agencies can do and how they must do it, covering rulemaking, enforcement, adjudication, and judicial review.
- **Agency** - A government body created by statute to carry out a defined mission, exercising powers Congress grants it.
- **Enabling statute** - The law that creates an agency, defines its mission, and grants its powers. Also called an organic statute.
- **Administrative Procedure Act (APA)** - The 1946 master statute setting uniform procedures for how federal agencies make rules, decide cases, and face judicial review.
- **Rulemaking** - The process an agency uses to write a regulation that applies broadly to everyone in a category, functioning like a statute.
- **Adjudication** - The process an agency uses to decide a specific case involving specific parties, functioning like a court proceeding.
- **Notice-and-comment rulemaking** - The standard rulemaking process under APA Section 553: publish a proposed rule, take public comments, then issue a final rule with an explanation.
- **Notice of Proposed Rulemaking (NPRM)** - The formal announcement in the Federal Register that an agency plans to issue a rule, including the proposed text and reasoning.
- **Federal Register** - The government's official daily publication where agencies announce proposed and final rules and other actions.
- **Formal rulemaking** - A trial-type rulemaking process with a hearing, testimony under oath, and cross-examination, required only when a statute clearly demands a decision "on the record after a hearing." Now nearly extinct.
- **Informal rulemaking** - The notice-and-comment process, called informal only in contrast to formal rulemaking. It produces the vast majority of federal rules.
- **Hybrid rulemaking** - A middle process created by specific statutes that requires more than notice and comment but less than a full formal hearing.
- **Logical outgrowth** - The requirement that a final rule stay close enough to the proposed rule that the public could reasonably have anticipated it, so the notice remains meaningful.
- **Legislative rule** - A rule that carries the force of law and creates new legal obligations. Must go through notice and comment. Also called a substantive rule.
- **Interpretive rule** - A rule that explains what an existing statute or regulation means, exempt from notice and comment.
- **General statement of policy** - An announcement of how an agency intends to exercise its discretion, exempt from notice and comment.
- **Good cause exemption** - The APA provision letting an agency skip notice and comment when it would be impracticable, unnecessary, or contrary to the public interest.
- **Interim final rule** - A rule that takes effect immediately without prior notice and comment, with the agency accepting comments afterward. Used under the good cause exemption.

- **Ossification** - The idea that rulemaking has become so slow and costly that agencies avoid it, reaching for guidance and other shortcuts instead.
- **Executive agency** - An agency whose head serves at the president's pleasure and can be removed at will. Changes direction with each administration.
- **Independent agency** - An agency run by a multimember commission whose members serve fixed terms and can be removed only for cause, designed to resist political pressure.
- **For-cause removal** - A statutory protection allowing an official to be fired only for reasons like inefficiency, neglect, or misconduct, not mere policy disagreement.
- **Cabinet department** - One of the fifteen major executive departments whose heads make up the president's cabinet.
- **Sub-agency** - A smaller agency nested inside a larger department, often with its own mission and leadership, like the FDA within Health and Human Services.
- **Appointments Clause** - The constitutional provision governing how federal officers are appointed, requiring Senate confirmation for principal officers.
- **Principal officer** - A high-level official, such as a cabinet secretary or agency head, who must be appointed by the president with Senate confirmation.
- **Inferior officer** - A lesser officer who can be appointed without Senate confirmation, by the president alone, the courts, or a department head.
- **Non-delegation doctrine** - The principle that Congress can't hand its lawmaking power to an agency. Enforced strictly only twice, both in 1935.
- **Intelligible principle** - The standard from J.W. Hampton (1928) allowing delegation as long as Congress gives the agency a clear enough guiding standard.
- **Fourth branch** - An informal label for the administrative state, reflecting how agencies combine legislative, executive, and judicial functions the Constitution kept separate.
- **Executive order** - A written command from the president to the executive branch that carries the force of law when it rests on constitutional or statutory authority.
- **Signing statement** - A statement issued when the president signs a bill, expressing the president's interpretation of the new law.
- **Statutory mandate** - A duty an enabling statute requires an agency to perform, often signaled by the word "shall," as opposed to discretion signaled by "may."
- **Delegated authority** - Power an agency holds because Congress granted it. The foundation of nearly everything agencies do.
- **Implied powers** - Powers reasonably necessary to carry out an agency's express powers, still traced back to the statute.
- **Inherent authority** - Power a body would hold simply by its nature, without any grant. Agencies don't have it.
- **Ultra vires** - Latin for "beyond the powers." Describes an agency action that exceeds its granted authority and can be struck down.
- **Judicial review** - The power of courts to examine agency action and strike it down if the agency exceeded its authority, ignored evidence, or skipped required procedures.
- **Standing** - The requirement that a plaintiff have a sufficient personal stake in a dispute to bring it into federal court.

- **Injury in fact** - A concrete, particularized harm that is actual or imminent. The first element of standing.
- **Causation** - The requirement that the plaintiff's injury be fairly traceable to the challenged agency action. The second element of standing.
- **Redressability** - The requirement that a favorable court decision would likely remedy the plaintiff's injury. The third element of standing.
- **Zone of interests** - A prudential test asking whether a plaintiff's interest is the kind the relevant statute was meant to protect.
- **Associational standing** - The doctrine letting an organization sue on behalf of its members when those members would have standing themselves.
- **Chevron deference** - The overruled 1984 doctrine requiring courts to accept an agency's reasonable interpretation of an ambiguous statute it administers.
- **Skidmore respect** - The weaker principle, surviving Chevron's fall, under which courts give an agency's interpretation weight based on how persuasive it is.
- **Auer deference** - Deference to an agency's interpretation of its own ambiguous regulation, narrowed sharply by Kisor v. Wilkie (2019).
- **Arbitrary and capricious** - The APA standard directing courts to set aside agency actions that lack reasoned support, ignore evidence, or fail to consider important factors.
- **Hard look review** - The practice, from State Farm, of courts examining whether an agency genuinely engaged with the evidence and alternatives before deciding.
- **Reasoned explanation** - The requirement that an agency articulate a rational connection between the facts it found and the choice it made, judged on the reasoning the agency actually gave.
- **Major questions doctrine** - The principle that on questions of vast economic and political significance, courts won't read a statute to grant agency power without a clear statement from Congress.
- **Exhaustion of administrative remedies** - The rule that a party generally must complete an agency's internal review process before seeking review in court.
- **Ripeness** - The doctrine asking whether a dispute has matured enough to be fit for judicial decision.
- **Finality** - The requirement that a court review only "final agency action," meaning a definitive decision rather than a tentative step.
- **Administrative law judge (ALJ)** - An official who presides over an agency's formal hearings, manages proceedings, and issues an initial decision the agency can review.
- **Decisional independence** - The insulation ALJs have, including for-cause removal and outside pay-setting, meant to let them decide cases honestly even against their own agency.
- **Separation of functions** - The APA safeguard keeping the people who investigated or prosecuted a case from also advising the decision-maker on it.
- **Ex parte communication** - A private, off-the-record contact between a decision-maker and one side about the merits of a case, prohibited in formal proceedings.
- **Consent decree** - A settlement entered as a court order, carrying the enforceability of a judicial judgment.

- **Civil penalty** - A monetary sanction for a violation, imposed without jail time or the full protections of criminal procedure. The workhorse of enforcement.
- **Disgorgement** - An order requiring a wrongdoer to give up profits gained from illegal conduct, meant to remove ill-gotten gains rather than to punish.
- **Public rights doctrine** - An exception allowing certain matters, like benefits and immigration, to be decided by agencies without juries. Read narrowly in Jarkesy.
- **Due process** - The constitutional guarantee that the government can't deprive a person of life, liberty, or property without fair procedure.
- **Property interest** - A protected interest, including benefits and entitlements a person has a legitimate claim to, that triggers due process before it's taken away.
- **Mathews balancing test** - The three-factor test weighing the private interest, the risk of error, and the government's burden to decide how much process is due.
- **Administrative subpoena** - An agency demand for documents or testimony, enforceable if the investigation is legitimate, relevant, and not unreasonably burdensome.
- **Closely regulated industry** - A field with a long history of pervasive regulation where agencies may conduct warrantless inspections because operators have reduced privacy expectations.
- **Cooperative federalism** - An arrangement where the federal government sets minimum standards and states run the actual programs, common in environmental regulation.
- **Disclosure-based regulation** - The securities-law approach of requiring companies to tell the truth about themselves and letting investors decide, rather than judging investment merit.
- **Congressional Review Act (CRA)** - The 1996 law giving Congress a fast, filibuster-proof way to cancel recent agency rules by joint resolution.
- **Appropriations rider** - A provision attached to a funding bill that directs or restricts how an agency can spend money, often used to block specific rules.
- **Inspector general** - An independent watchdog inside an agency who audits programs and investigates misconduct, reporting to both the agency head and Congress.
- **Freedom of Information Act (FOIA)** - The 1966 law giving any person the right to request federal agency records, with the burden on the government to justify withholding.
- **Deliberative process privilege** - A FOIA exemption protecting the internal give-and-take of agency decision-making, like drafts and recommendations.
- **Vaughn index** - A detailed list an agency must provide in FOIA litigation describing each withheld document and why an exemption applies.
- **Whistleblower** - An employee who discloses wrongdoing and is protected from retaliation for doing so.
- **Qui tam** - A provision of the False Claims Act letting private individuals sue on the government's behalf to recover funds lost to fraud, sharing in the recovery.
- **Legislative veto** - A device, struck down in INS v. Chadha (1983), by which Congress reserved power to overturn agency actions by resolution without full lawmaking.

Works Cited & Recommended Readings

Cases

A.L.A. Schechter Poultry Corp. v. United States, 295 U.S. 495 (1935).

Abbott Laboratories v. Gardner, 387 U.S. 136 (1967).

Bi-Metallic Investment Co. v. State Board of Equalization, 239 U.S. 441 (1915).

Biden v. Nebraska, 600 U.S. 477 (2023).

Chevron U.S.A., Inc. v. Natural Resources Defense Council, Inc., 467 U.S. 837 (1984).

Citizens to Preserve Overton Park v. Volpe, 401 U.S. 402 (1971).

Corner Post, Inc. v. Board of Governors of the Federal Reserve System, 144 S. Ct. 2440 (2024).

Department of Commerce v. New York, 588 U.S. 752 (2019).

FDA v. Brown & Williamson Tobacco Corp., 529 U.S. 120 (2000).

Free Enterprise Fund v. Public Company Accounting Oversight Board, 561 U.S. 477 (2010).

Goldberg v. Kelly, 397 U.S. 254 (1970).

Gundy v. United States, 588 U.S. 128 (2019).

Heckler v. Chaney, 470 U.S. 821 (1985).

Humphrey's Executor v. United States, 295 U.S. 602 (1935).

J.W. Hampton, Jr. & Co. v. United States, 276 U.S. 394 (1928).

Kisor v. Wilkie, 588 U.S. 558 (2019).

Londoner v. Denver, 210 U.S. 373 (1908).

Loper Bright Enterprises v. Raimondo, 144 S. Ct. 2244 (2024).

Lucia v. SEC, 585 U.S. 237 (2018).

Lujan v. Defenders of Wildlife, 504 U.S. 555 (1992).

Marbury v. Madison, 5 U.S. (1 Cranch) 137 (1803).

Marshall v. Barlow's, Inc., 436 U.S. 307 (1978).

Massachusetts v. EPA, 549 U.S. 497 (2007).

Mathews v. Eldridge, 424 U.S. 319 (1976).

Morrison v. Olson, 487 U.S. 654 (1988).

Motor Vehicle Manufacturers Association v. State Farm Mutual Automobile Insurance Co., 463 U.S. 29 (1983).

Myers v. United States, 272 U.S. 52 (1926).

National Federation of Independent Business v. Department of Labor, OSHA, 595 U.S. 109 (2022).

SEC v. Jarkesy, 144 S. Ct. 2117 (2024).

Seila Law LLC v. Consumer Financial Protection Bureau, 591 U.S. 197 (2020).

United States v. Florida East Coast Railway Co., 410 U.S. 224 (1973).

United States v. Mead Corp., 533 U.S. 218 (2001).

Vermont Yankee Nuclear Power Corp. v. Natural Resources Defense Council, 435 U.S. 519 (1978).

West Virginia v. EPA, 597 U.S. 697 (2022).

Whitman v. American Trucking Associations, 531 U.S. 457 (2001).

Youngstown Sheet & Tube Co. v. Sawyer, 343 U.S. 579 (1952).

Statutes, Regulations, and Executive Orders

Administrative Procedure Act, 5 U.S.C. §§ 551–559, 701–706 (1946).

Clean Air Act, 42 U.S.C. §§ 7401–7671q.

Congressional Review Act, 5 U.S.C. §§ 801–808 (1996).

Dodd-Frank Wall Street Reform and Consumer Protection Act, Pub. L. No. 111-203, 124 Stat. 1376 (2010).

Exec. Order No. 12866, 3 C.F.R. 638 (1993).

Freedom of Information Act, 5 U.S.C. § 552 (1966).

Inspector General Act of 1978, 5 U.S.C. §§ 401–424.

Interstate Commerce Act, ch. 104, 24 Stat. 379 (1887).

Occupational Safety and Health Act of 1970, 29 U.S.C. §§ 651–678.

Securities Exchange Act of 1934, 15 U.S.C. §§ 78a et seq.

Whistleblower Protection Act of 1989, 5 U.S.C. § 2302.

Books and Articles

Bradford, A. (2020). *The Brussels effect: How the European Union rules the world*. Oxford University Press.

Breyer, S. G., Stewart, R. B., Sunstein, C. R., Vermeule, A., & Herz, M. (2022). *Administrative law and regulatory policy: Problems, text, and cases* (9th ed.). Wolters Kluwer.

Coglianese, C., & Lehr, D. (2017). Regulating by robot: Administrative decision making in the machine-learning era. *Georgetown Law Journal, 105*(5), 1147–1223.

Engstrom, D. F., Ho, D. E., Sharkey, C. M., & Cuéllar, M.-F. (2020). *Government by algorithm: Artificial intelligence in federal administrative agencies*. Administrative Conference of the United States.

Kagan, E. (2001). Presidential administration. *Harvard Law Review, 114*(8), 2245–2385.

Mashaw, J. L. (2012). *Creating the administrative constitution: The lost one hundred years of American administrative law*. Yale University Press.

Metzger, G. E. (2017). Foreword: 1930s redux: The administrative state under siege. *Harvard Law Review, 131*(1), 1–95.

Pierce, R. J., Jr. (2010). *Administrative law treatise* (5th ed.). Aspen Publishers.

Rabin, R. L. (1986). Federal regulation in historical perspective. *Stanford Law Review, 38*(5), 1189–1326.

Strauss, P. L. (2016). *Administrative justice in the United States* (3rd ed.). Carolina Academic Press.

Sunstein, C. R., & Vermeule, A. (2020). *Law and Leviathan: Redeeming the administrative state.* Harvard University Press.

Recommended Readings

Carpenter, D. (2010). *Reputation and power: Organizational image and pharmaceutical regulation at the FDA.* Princeton University Press.

> This is the definitive account of how the FDA built its authority, and it gives full context to the thalidomide episode that opens this book. If you want to understand how one agency actually earned the power it wields, start here.

Breyer, S. (1993). *Breaking the vicious circle: Toward effective risk regulation.* Harvard University Press.

> Written by a Supreme Court Justice before he joined the Court, this short book explains why agencies regulate risk the way they do and where the process goes wrong. It's clear, practical, and refreshingly honest about the trade-offs.

Bradford, A. (2020). *The Brussels effect: How the European Union rules the world.* Oxford University Press.

> A readable account of how European regulations quietly become global standards through market pressure rather than treaties, which is the international dimension Chapter 9 only introduces.

Mashaw, J. L. (2012). *Creating the administrative constitution: The lost one hundred years of American administrative law.* Yale University Press.

> Mashaw recovers the forgotten history of administrative governance in the century before the New Deal, showing that the regulatory state has far deeper roots than most people assume.

Sunstein, C. R. (2013). *Simpler: The future of government.* Simon & Schuster.

> Sunstein ran the White House office that reviews federal regulations, and this book pulls back the curtain on how cost-benefit analysis and regulatory review actually work inside the executive branch. It pairs well with the material on Executive Order 12866.

www.ingramcontent.com/pod-product-compliance
Lightning Source LLC
LaVergne TN
LVHW010731061126
851857LV00014B/1431
9798900421339